MEDIEVAL LOCAL RECORDS

A Reading Aid

K. C. NEWTON

County Archivist of Essex

Helps for Students of History
No. 83

The Historical Association

ACKNOWLEDGMENTS

I am grateful to my colleagues, the City Archivist of Coventry (Plate XII) and the County Archivists of Gloucestershire (Plate IV), Hertfordshire (Plate V), Northamptonshire (Plate VI) and Staffordshire (Plate II), for selecting suitable manuscripts from their collection and for arranging the provision of excellent photographs. The remaining Plates are taken from sources in the Essex Record Office and warm thanks are due to Mr. N. Hammond, senior photographic assistant there, for the care bestowed upon the making of the prints. I am indebted to Professor H. R. Loyn, D.Litt., Dr. C. H. Knowles and Mr. J. L. Kirby, M.A., F.S.A., Librarian, The History Faculty Library, Oxford, for reading my work in typescript; it has benefited in general and in points of detail from their constructive criticism. To my wife I express gratitude for typing the text and admiration for her patience and skill in deciphering the most difficult hand of all – my own. For those errors that remain in print I am solely responsible.

K.C.N.

We are grateful for a donation of £25 from the Friends of Historic Essex towards the expense of publication. Those wishing to continue their studies into a later period are advised to consult H.82: F. G. Emmison, *How to Read Local Archives, 1500–1700* (2nd. ed. 1967).

ISBN 085278 039 7

Printed in Great Britain by The Chameleon Press Limited, 5-25 Burr Road, Wandsworth, London SW18 4SG

MEDIEVAL LOCAL RECORDS

In local record offices there is a vast body of records dating from before 1500, the detailed content of which remains and will remain in the foreseeable future for the most part unavailable to the local historian, unless he is practised in palaeography and has a basic knowledge of Latin and Anglo-French. Knowledge of the latter language is much less important as the number of local records written in it is relatively small. Many charters may have been calendared, so that reference to the originals is normally unnecessary, but very few manor court rolls or bailiffs' accounts, or other lengthy records in long series, have received such detailed cataloguing and will by their nature remain more or less brief entries in summary lists. Learning to read the old scripts in which the earliest documents likely to be found in a local record office are written is not inherently difficult but is dependent primarily on practice, practice and more practice, with some guidance to avoid consistency of error. It is to this end that this little book has been prepared as a practical aid.

The scripts employed in the documents reproduced in the illustrations, with the exception of Plate I which is an example of Book Hands (see below), are termed Court Hands or sometimes Charter Hands. Strictly, Court Hands are those which were evolved and employed in the central courts of law from the 12th century onwards, each court developing its own characteristic script. But by general consent the term is used to cover those hands in which the vast majority of public and private, central and local records was written. Both Court Hands and Book Hands had a common origin in the Caroline Minuscule which was current from the 8th to the 12th century. Latin charters of the Anglo-Saxon period provide examples of the Caroline Minuscule: the vernacular (often used in such charters to describe the bounds of the lands granted) was written in the native script.[1] By the end of the 12th century Court Hand was quite distinct from Book Hand which continued to be used for liturgical manuscripts and learned and literary works.

The principal characteristic of Court Hand is that it is cursive, though not to the same extent as modern handwriting except on the rare occasions when it is written quickly and not in accordance with rule. While essentially an utilitarian hand for writing administrative documents – court rolls, rentals, surveys, charters and the like – the ever-growing output of which made speed in writing an essential qualification for a scribe, nevertheless Court Hand achieved a remarkable beauty of its own, notably in the earlier part of the 14th century, which led to its use for writing literary works. But in common with so much else in the medieval world Court Hand declined in the 15th century and there is usually little elegance to be seen in documents written towards and at the end of our period, particularly in those of local origin.

Like the language to which it seeks to give visual expression, handwriting is subject to an evolutionary development even when written in accordance with strict rules. It follows therefore that it is possible – within certain limits – to date documents from the evidence of the scripts. Even a general comparison of the documents reproduced here will demonstrate this point. The importance of this is seen when it is remembered that private charters rarely have a dating clause before about the last decade of the 13th century: the character of the writing may be the only means of approximately dating such charters.

Distinguishing characteristics of Court Hands at various stages of their development will be dealt with under the *approximate* dates within which they fall. Due allowance, more particularly perhaps with local charters, must be made for the possibility that the scribe is either an old man writing in the fashionable script of his youth or has been taught an old-fashioned script by his teacher. An expert in palaeography can mis-date a document by as much as fifty years or more if he makes use of only the evidence of the handwriting.[2] But in the absence of other evidence it is surely far better to make a reasoned attempt than merely to write 'date unknown'.

ABBREVIATIONS

Even when armed with a basic knowledge of Latin and a medieval wordlist, the newcomer to ancient documents is faced with the problem of abbreviations, for he or she will find that many words are shortened by contraction and suspension indicated by special signs and superior letters. It is worth remembering at all times that particularly puzzling words in a manuscript may well be the result of a combination of these methods of abbreviation (e.g. Plate I, l.5, *quicumque*). Again the solution to the problem is largely a matter of familiarization through practice.

In addition to the *Table of signs* (loose sheet) and notes the reader's attention is drawn to particular examples given in the notes to the documents used as illustrations.

SIGNS OF CONTRACTION AND SUSPENSION (*see Table of signs*)

1[3] written above a letter = (i) the omission of *m* or *n*; (ii) the omission of *er* when drawn through the head of a tall letter (e.g., *h* or *b*); (iii) a general sign of contraction or suspension. Note that the dotted form (found 14th century onwards) becomes very common in the 15th century as a general sign of abbreviation.

2 above the line = (i) *er, re, ir, or*; (ii) a general sign of contraction or suspension.

3 above the line = *us, os*; on the line = *con*. Note *h* and *p*+sign above the line = *h(ujus)* and *p(ost)* respectively.

4 = *es, is*. Unusual before 1300. Much used in English documents to denote final *es*. At first also used as a general sign of suspension, particularly after *g* and *t*, but becomes restricted to representing *es, is*.

1. For examples, see *Facsimiles of Ancient Charters in the British Museum* (parts 1–4, London, 1873–8).
2. Other supporting evidence should, of course, always be sought first.
3. This number gives reference to the appropriate symbol in the *Table of signs*, enclosed as a loose leaf in this pamphlet.

5 above the line = *ur*. Note that it sometimes represents *tur, atur, itur*, etc., *i.e.* the third person singular passive ending of verbs. The sign stems from the round *r*.

6 = (i) *et, ue, us*; (ii) *que, bus*; (iii) a general sign of contraction. Note that the z-like form is the cursive of the 'semi-colon' form, which is unusual after 1200.

7 = *est*. Unusual after 1200.

8 = the Tironian[1] sign for *et* or *and*. Over the centuries this sign takes many forms (see illustrations and notes thereto). Note that the ampersand (& = *et* or *and*) is not often met with in our period.

MODIFICATION OF LETTERS TO INDICATE ABBREVIATION (*see Table of signs*)

The examples given in the *Table* are the most common.

1 = p(re). Not found in Court Hand after about 1200.

2 = p(re). Supersedes 1 in Court Hand.

3 = p(er), p(ar), p(or). 4 = p(ro). Liable to confusion with 3.

5 = q(ue). 6 = q(uod). 7 = q(ue). 8 = q(uia).

9 (*i.e.* a round *r* modified by a vertical stroke) = (i) a general sign of contraction; (ii) r(um). Hence *Sarum* incorrectly for *Sarisburiensis*.

10 (*i.e.* a long *s* modified by a horizontal stroke = s(er).) Found from the 14th century onwards, mostly in French and vernacular documents, but not very common until the 15th century.

ABBREVIATION BY SUPERIOR LETTERS

Suspension and contraction may also be made by writing a letter above the line. Normally this indicates that two or more letters (of which the superior letter is one) have been omitted from the word on the line. Thus qᵃlis = q(u)*a*lis, qⁿor = q(u)*a*(tu)or. Sometimes a superior letter indicates that another has been left out from the word. By this method *u* after *q* is omitted by placing the following vowel above the line, as in the two examples above; *r* before a vowel is omitted by placing the vowel above the line (pⁱor = p(r)*i*or, intᵒ = int(r)*o*). Superior *r* indicates the omission of *u* (tʳnus = t(u)*r*nus; superior *c* the omission of a preceding vowel (nᶜ = n(e)*c*, hᶜ = h(o)*c*). Considerable abbreviation may be effected by the use of superior letters, as pᵗ = p(otes)*t*, mʳ = m(agiste)*r*, quaʳ = qua(lite)*r*. Note also gʳ = (i)g(itu)*r*, gᵃ = (er)g*a*. Sometimes a whole syllable is written above the line, as mᵈᵘᵐ = m(emoran)*dum*; and the superior letter itself may bear a sign of contraction or suspension.

RUNES (*see Table of signs*)

Since vernacular documents of the 12th–14th century are rarely found in local record offices, the student will usually find runes occurring only in place-names and in later copies of ancient documents.

1 = *th*. This often appears incorrectly as a normal *d*. (This has led to the modern controversy whether 'the Rodings' or 'the Roothings' is the correct spelling for the name of a group of Essex villages.)

2 = *th*, and is known as 'thorn'. This is found during the whole of our period. At first (12th century) it resembles a *þ*, but then becomes difficult to distinguish from a *y* (*y* usually has a dot or accent above it in the 13th and 14th century, but this becomes less common in the 15th century and 'thorn' is written as *y* giving the well-known *ye* for *the*). See Plate IX for examples.

3 = Saxon *w*, and is known as 'wen'. It occurs only in pre-13th century documents or later copies thereof.

Note also 4. This is not a rune but a Saxon **g** (known as 'yogh'), which in sound was between *g* and *y*. By the 14th century its written form is usually indistinguishable from *z* (*cf.* the Scottish name Menzies). See Plate IX for examples.

PUNCTUATION

In the 11th and 12th centuries the full stop was used to mark both the complete sentence and lesser pauses. In the same period a mark resembling an inverted semicolon was also employed to indicate an intermediate as well as a final pause. In Plates I and II, it will be seen, the scribes have generally used the full stop to mark all pauses, but each charter contains one example of the inverted semicolon (Plate I, l.3, after *salute*; Plate II, l.10 l.3, after *suis*). One may also notice in Plate I, l.5, the usual practice of enclosing Roman numerals between two full stops (see also Plate II, l.10, Plate III, l.5, and Plate IV throughout). In ecclesiastical and royal documents it was common to represent the names of kings, prelates, great magnates, and other well known persons merely by their initial letters enclosed between two full points, or in the case of the highest personages by the two stops only. The absence of even the initial letter does *not* mean that the name was unknown but on the contrary that it was so well known as to render mention of it superfluous; t was a mark of honour. For obvious reasons this is rarely found in local charters. Where a full stop appears neither to separate clauses grammatically nor to indicate a 'natural' pause if the document were read aloud, it may well be that it marks the point where the scribe rested his pen for a moment!

In the latter part of the 13th century an oblique dash (/), often quite lightly made (see Plate V, l.4, after *altera*), begins to be used for shorter pauses

1. Tiro, the inventor of this form of shorthand, was the freedman secretary of Cicero.

and in time almost entirely replaces the full stop for this purpose. Less use is also made of the inverted semicolon, but when it is employed it may be written currently to form a single stroke which can lead to confusion with letter *i*. In the 15th century a stroke may be found in combination with a full stop to mark a complete sentence or the end of a whole document. Plate VI provides examples of this, the inverted semicolon and the oblique stroke.

By the 15th century a tendency towards less and less punctuation in formal instruments such as charters often reaches the ultimate, and as the century progresses more and more manuscripts will be found devoid of it; correspondingly greater care is usually taken to introduce a fresh clause with a capital letter (see, for example, Plate X).

NOTE ON THE FORM OF TRANSCRIPTS

The transcripts of the documents which follow the plates are exact and line for line. Abbreviations are extended or expanded, the letters omitted being supplied in round brackets. Superscript letters are printed in *italics*. Where extension or expansion is doubtful or impossible this is denoted by an apostrophe. *ff* has been printed F and capital I for J according to modern usage. The translations have been kept as literal as possible so that they may be easily related to the transcripts.

A NOTE OF WARNING

To facilitate learning and practice for the beginner using this pamphlet only formal documents, more or less well-written and unfaded, have been selected. However, it must be pointed out that by no means all medieval local records are so neat and readable. For example, it may be necessary to read the draft of a 15th-century manor court roll hurriedly written on paper now tattered because the fair engrossment on parchment has not survived; glosses may have been scrawled in the margin which greatly add to the understanding of an otherwise excellently written manuscript; or a charter may have become so faded that its words may be read only under an ultra-violet lamp – and then with much eye-strain and exercise of the imagination. But these are merely further challenges to be met and overcome.

Charters written in Book Hands continue to be found until the end of this period (see Plate I). At the same time Charter and Court Hands are developing (Plate II). It will be seen that the latter's distinguishing characteristics are (i) an exaggeration of the ascenders and descenders of letters, the ascenders curving forward, the descenders backward, and of the signs of contraction and suspension; (ii) the tops of the letters *b*, *h*, *l* and *I* are split into a notch or hook; (iii) capital letters are more elaborate.

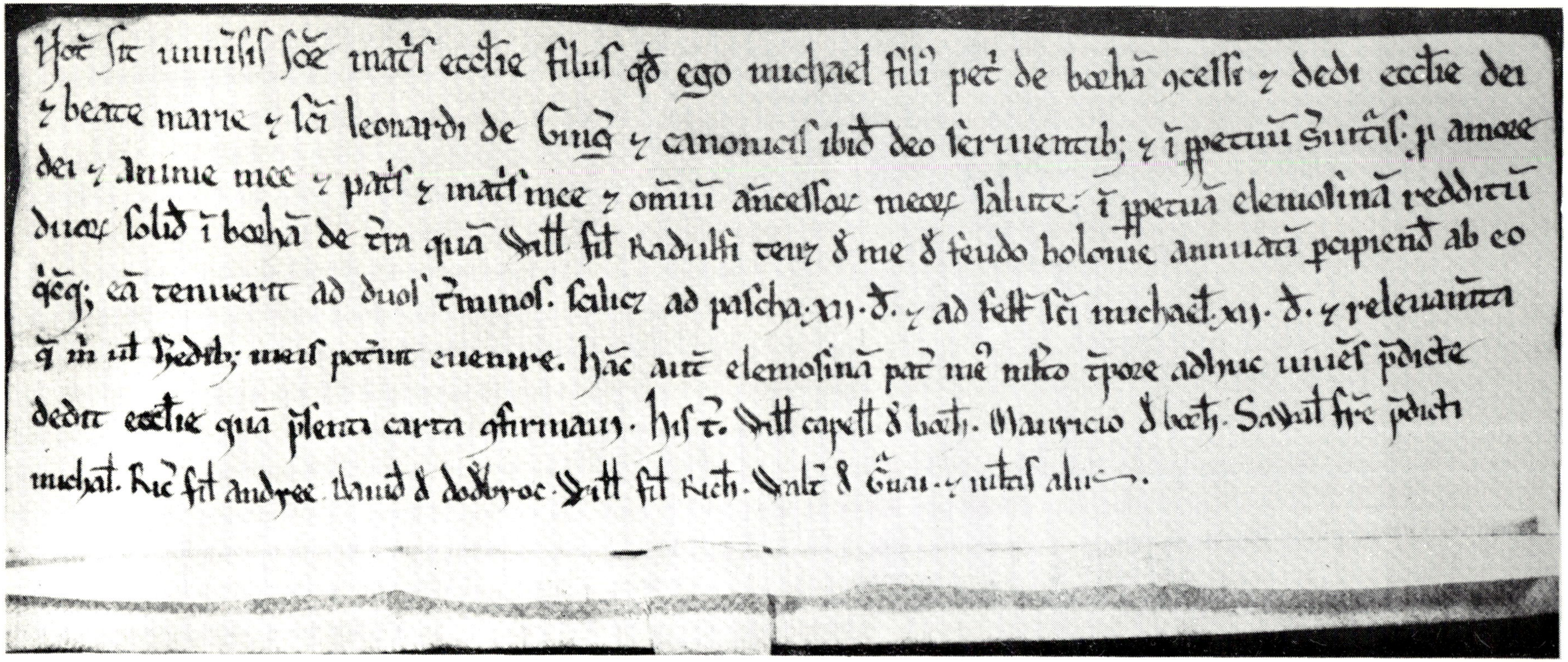

PLATE I. GRANT OF RENT IN BOREHAM, ESSEX, TO THOBY PRIORY, *c.* 1185

[Essex R.O., D/DP T1/124]   *Facsimile*

PLATE I. GRANT OF RENT IN BOREHAM, ESSEX, TO THOBY PRIORY, *c.* 1185

1. Not(um) sit uniu(er)sis[1] s(an)c(t)e mat(r)*is* eccl(es)ie filiis q(uo)d ego michael fili(us) pet(r)*i* de borha(m) (con)cessi (et)[2] dedi eccl(es)ie dei

2. (et) beate marie (et) s(an)c(t)i leonardi de Ging' (et) canonicis ibid(em) deo seruientib(us)[3] (et) i(n) p(er)petuu(m) s(er)uit(ur)is.[4] p(ro) amore

3. dei (et) anime mee (et) pat(r)*is* (et) mat(r)*is* mee (et) om(n)iu(m) an(te)cessor(um) meor(um) salute⁊   i(n) p(er)petua(m) elemosina(m) redditu(m)

4. duor(um) solid(orum) i(n) borha(m) de t(er)ra qua(m) Will(elmus) fil(ius) Radulfi ten(et) d(e)[5] me d(e) feudo bolonie annuati(m) p(er)cipiend(um) ab eo

5. q(u)*ic*(um)q(ue)[6] ea(m) tenuerit ad duos t(er)minos. scilic(et) ad pascha .xij. d(enarios). (et) ad fest(um) s(an)c(t)i michael(is) .xij. d(enarios). (et) releuam(en)ta

6. q(ue) m(ih)*i*[7] u(e)l[8] h(er)edib(us) meis pot(er)int euenire. ha(n)c aut(em) elemosina(m) pat(er) me(us) m(u)lto[9] t(em)pore adhuc uiue(n)s p(re)dicte

7. dedit eccl(es)ie qua(m) p(re)senti carta (con)firmaui. His t(estibus). Will(elmo) capell(ano) d(e) borh(am). Mauricio d(e) borh(am). Sawal(o) fr(atr)e p(re)dicti

8. micha(e)l(is). Ric(ardo) fil(io) andree. Dauid' d(e) dod(e)broc. Will(elmo) fil(io) Rich(erij). Walt(ero) d(e) G(ur)nai.[10] (et) m(u)ltis aliis.[11]

Translation

Be it known to all the sons of Holy Mother Church that I, Michael son of Peter of Boreham, have granted and given to the church of God and of the Blessed Mary and of St. Leonard of 'Ging' (Mountnessing) and to the canons who serve and will serve God there for ever, for the love of God and the salvation of the souls of me, my father and mother and all my ancestors, in frank almoign, the rent of two shillings in Boreham from the land which William son of Ralph holds of me of the fee of Boulogne, to be received annually from whomsoever will hold it at the two terms, to wit, at Easter 12 pence and at the Feast of Saint Michael 12 pence, and the reliefs which may fall to me or my heirs. These alms, moreover, my father gave long ago in his own lifetime to the aforesaid church, which I have confirmed by the present charter. These being witnesses, William, chaplain of Boreham, Maurice of Boreham, Sawal, brother of the aforesaid Michael, Richard son of Andrew, David of 'Dodebroc', William son of Riquier, Walter of 'Gurnai' and many others.

NOTE

1. Form of sign for *er* at this time. Also commonly used as a general sign of abbreviation (see *Ging'*, l.2, and *t(estibus)*, l.7).
2. Form of Tironian sign for *et*.
3. Special sign for *us* like a semi-colon still in use.
4. Form of special sign for *ur*.
5. Form of sign abbreviating *de*. A simple stroke through the ascender of the *d* becomes more common.
6. Or q(u)*ic*(un)q(ue).
7. Or m(ich)*i*.
8. That *u* is more common than *v* as an initial letter in the 12th century; *v* medially is not found before the 15th century and then only rarely.
9. Sign denoting omission of *u* before *l*. This is uncommon but may be found in documents as late as *c.* 1275.
10. Possibly G(ur)uai.
11. Final *s* written in the form of a flourish.

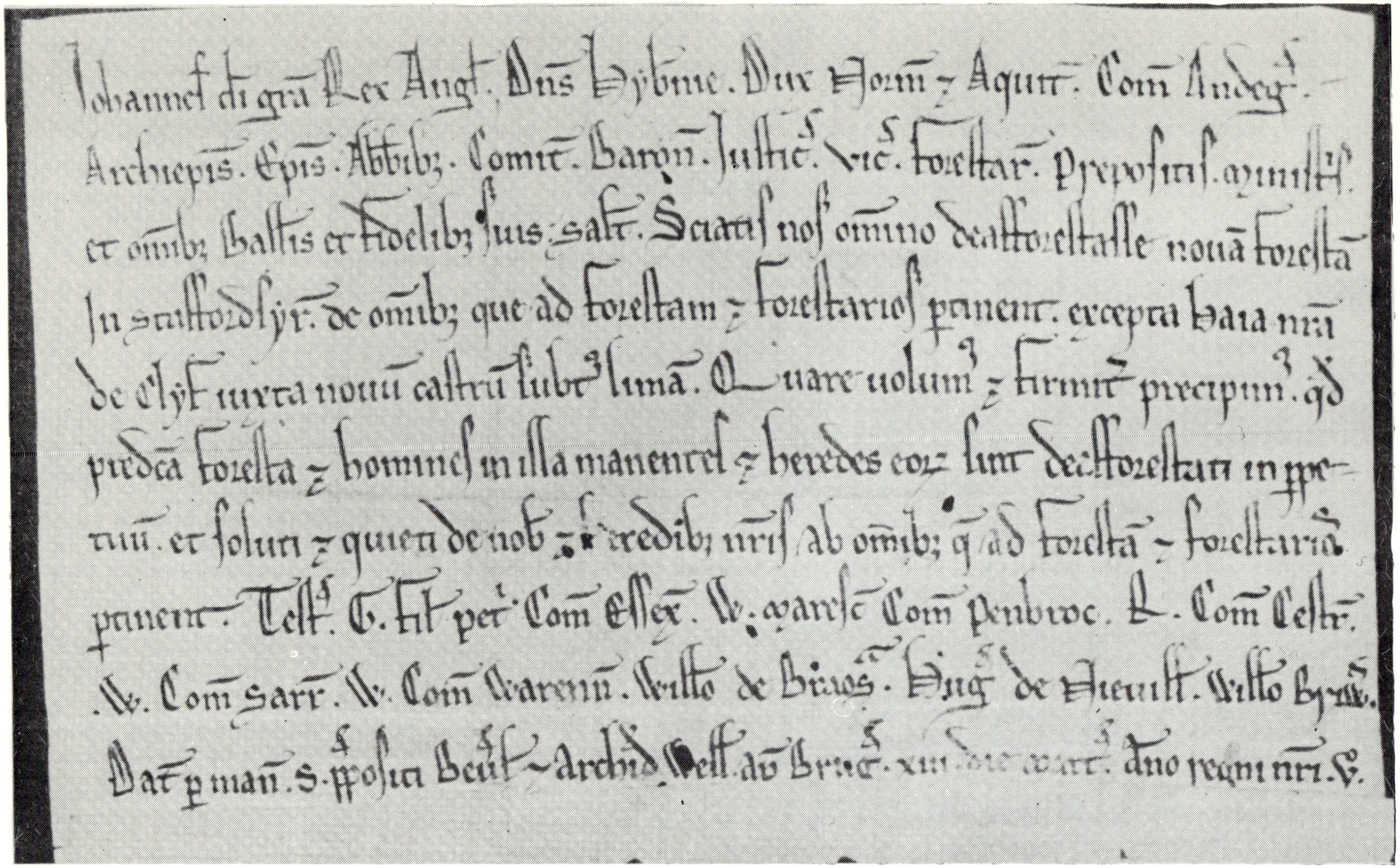

Iohannes di gra Rex Angl. Dns Hybnie. Dux Norm z Aquit. Com Andeg.
Archiepis. Epis. Abbibz. Comit. Baron. Justic. Vic. Forestar. Prepositis. ministris.
et omnibz ballis et fidelibz suis: salt. Sciatis nos omnino deafforestasse nouā forestā
In staffordsyr. de omnibz que ad forestam z forestarios ptinent. excepta haia nri
de Clyf iuxta nouū castrū sub lima. Quare volum z firmit precipim. qd
predca foresta z homines in illa manentes z heredes eoz sint deafforestati in ppe-
tuū. et soluti z quieti de nob z heredibz nris ab omibz q ad forestā z forestarios
ptinent. Test. G. fil pet Com Essex. W. mares Com Penbroc. R. Com Cestr.
W. Com Sarr. W. Com Warenn. Willo de Braos. Hug de Neuill. Willo briwerr.
Dat p man. S. ppositi Beuul z archid. Well. ap Brug. xiii die Mart. Anno regni nri. V.

PLATE II. CHARTER OF KING JOHN DISAFFORESTING THE NEW FOREST, STAFFORDSHIRE, 1204

[Staffs. R.O., D938/7969] *Facsimile*

1. Johannes d(e)i gr(ati)a Rex Angl(ie). D(omi)n(u)s Hyb(er)nie. Dux Norm(annie) (et)[1] Aquit(annie). Com(es) Andeg(auie).[2]
2. Archiep(iscop)is. Ep(iscop)is. Abb(at)ib(us).[3] Comit(ibus). Baron(ibus). Justic(iis). vic(ecomitibus). forestar(iis).[4] Prepositis. Minist(r)is.
3. et om(n)ib(us) Ball(iu)is et fidelib(us) suis꞉ Sal(u)t(em). Sciatis nos om(n)ino deafforestasse noua(m) foresta(m)
4. In Staffordsyr'. de om(n)ib(us) que ad forestam (et) forestarios p(er)tinent. excepta Haia n(ost)ra
5. de Clyf iuxta nouu(m) castru(m) subt(us) lima(m). Quare uolum(us) (et) firmit(er) precipim(us). q(uo)d
6. pred(i)c(t)a foresta (et) homines in illa manentes (et) heredes eor(um) sint deafforestati in p(er)pe-
7. tuu(m). et soluti (et) quieti de nob(is) (et) heredib(us) n(ost)ris ab om(n)ib(us) q(ue) ad foresta(m) (et) forestarios
8. p(er)tinent. Test(ibus). G(alfrido). fil(io) pet(r)i Com(ite) Essex(ie). W(illelmo). Maresc(allo) Com(ite) Penbroc. R(anulfo). Com(ite) Cestr(ie).
9. .W(illelmo). Com(ite) Sarr(esberie). W(illelmo). Com(ite) Warenn(ie). Wi'l(elm)o de Braosa.[5] Hug(one) de Nieuill(a). Will(elm)o Briw(er).
10. Dat(a) p(er) man(us). S(imonis). p(re)positi Beu(er)l(aci) (et) archid(iaconi) Well(ensis) ap(ud) Brug(am). xiii. die Marc(ii). an(n)o regni
    n(ost)ri .v̊[6]

Translation

John by grace of God King of England, Lord of Ireland, Duke of Normandy and Aquitaine, Court of Anjou, to his archbishops, bishops, abbots, earls, barons, justices, sheriffs, foresters, reeves, ministers and to all bailiffs and faithful subjects greetings. Know ye that we have completely disafforested the New Forest in Staffordshire of all things that pertain to forest and foresters, except our enclosure of 'Clyf' near to Newcastle-under-Lyme. Wherefore it is our will and we strongly command that the aforesaid forest and the men dwelling there and their heirs be disafforested for ever and released and quit of us and our heirs from all things that pertain to the forest and foresters. Witnesses, Geoffrey son of Peter, Earl of Essex, William Marshall, Earl of Pembroke, Ranulf, Earl of Chester, William, Earl of Salisbury, Earl William of Warenne, William de Broase, Hugh de Neville, William Briwer. Given by the hands of Simon, Provost of Beverley and Archdeacon of Wells, at Bridgenorth on the 13th day of March in the 5th year of our reign.

NOTE

1. The form of the Tironian sign for *et*.
2. The elaborate form that the general sign of suspension takes here and elsewhere in the document.
3. The contraction sign for *us* is the cursive of the 'semi-colon' form seen in Plate I.
4. Until the latter years of the 13th century it is virtually impossible to tell whether a capital or a small *f* is intended, except perhaps by the comparative sizes of the characters. Thereafter the capital is usually represented by *ff*. In this charter note that one form of *f* is used initially (except in *forestarios*, l.7) and terminally (*Clyf*, l.5) and another form medially (e.g., *deafforestasse*, l.3).
5. The superior *a* differs from *a* on the line. It is in effect an archaic open *a* closed by a horizontal stroke. It may be used just as as spacesaver (as here), but may also indicate abbreviation (e.g. ac(r)*as* in Plate III, l.2).
6. For an unextended transcript of the enrolment of this charter, see *Rotuli Chartarum in Turri Londinensi*, vol. i, part i, 1199–1216 (Record Commission, 1837), p. 122.

Early in the 13th century there are pronounced changes in the style of handwriting. Its main characteristics are (i) a smaller hand; (ii) the splitting of the tops of *b*, *h* and *l* becomes more pronounced, the right-hand hook often being exaggerated into a loop coming down (almost) to the line, and in the more cursive scripts the loop is formed by running on from the previous letter as in a modern hand; (iii) the descender of initial capital *I* curves round to meet the left-hand hook of the split top; (iv) the head of *d* turns over to make a complete loop and the head of long *s* is also exaggerated; (v) a headless *a* with lengthened down-stroke, so as to resemble a *q* is found, while the head of the headed *a* tends to be brought down to meet the first loop (this becomes the most common form); (vi) horizontal and oblique strokes of letters and signs of abbreviation become thicker than the down-strokes, though these too tend to become thicker, presenting a wedge-shaped appearance.

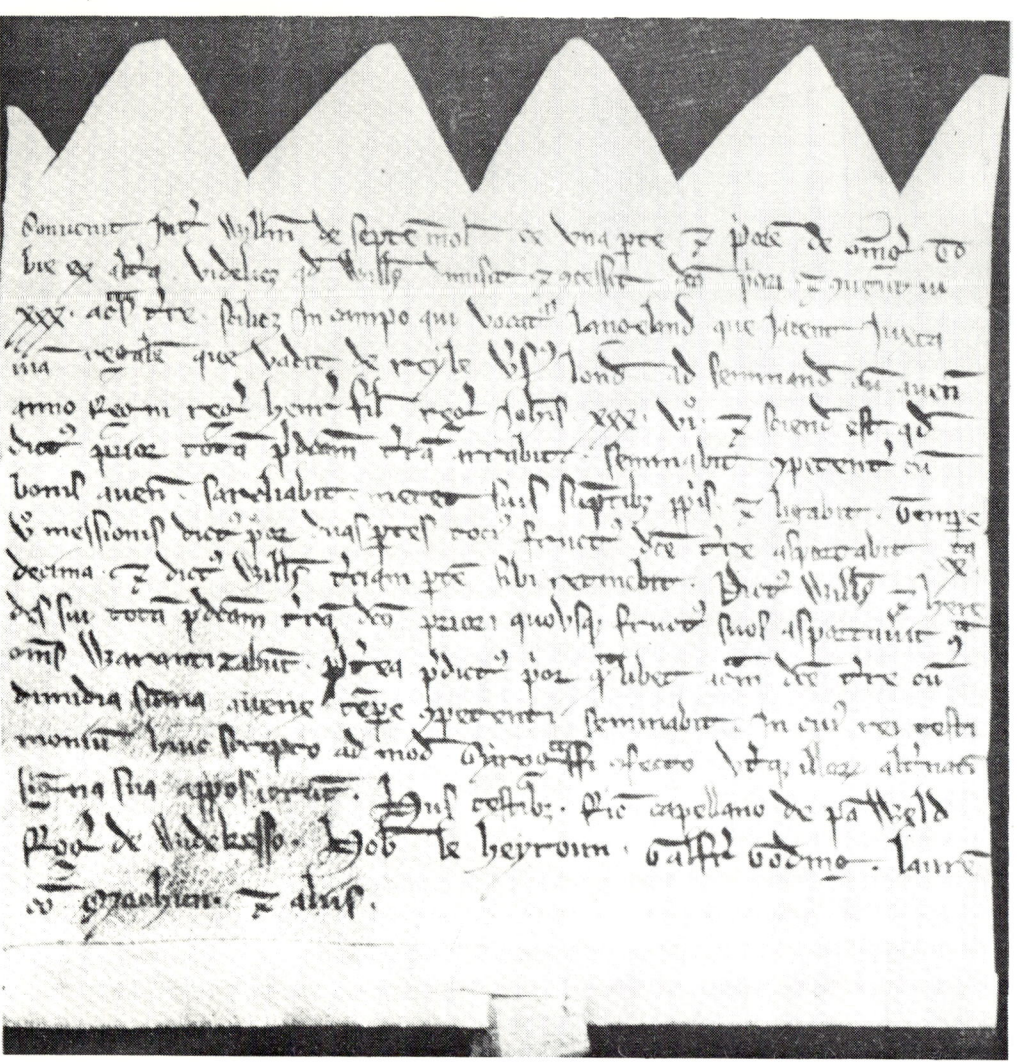

PLATE III. AGREEMENT TO LEASE LAND IN (?)MOUNTNESSING, ESSEX, *c.* 1251

[Essex R.O., D/DP T1/36]

Facsimile

PLATE III. AGREEMENT TO LEASE LAND IN (?)MOUNTNESSING, ESSEX, *c.* 1251

1. Conuenit Int(er) Will(elmu)m de septe(m) mol(endinis) ex vna[1] p(ar)te (et) P(r)*i*ore(m) de Ging' To[2]
2. bie ex alt(er)a.[3] videlic(et) q(uo)d Will(elmu)s dimisit (et) (con)cessit d(i)c(t)o p(r)iori (et) (con)uentui
3. xxx. ac(r)*as* t(er)re. scilic(et) In campo qui vocat(ur)[4] lanoeland que Iacent Iuxta
4. uia(m) regale(m) que vadit de reyle v(er)s(us) lond' ad seminand(um) cu(m) auen(is)
5. anno Regni reg(is) henr(ici) fil(ii) reg(is) Joh(ann)is .xxx. v̊i. (et) sciend(um) est q(uo)d
6. dict(us) prior tota(m) p(re)d(i)c(t)am t(er)ra(m) arrabit. seminabit (com)petent(er) cu(m)
7. bonis auen(is). sarcliabit. metet suis su(m)ptib(us) p(ro)p(r)iis. (et) ligabit. Temp(or)e
8. v(er)*o* messionis dict(us) p(r)*i*or duas p(ar)tes toci(us) fruct(us) d(i)c(t)e t(er)re asportabit ex(cep)*ta*
9. decima. (et) dict(us) Will(elmu)s t(er)ciam p(ar)te(m) sibi retinebit. Dict(us) Will(elmu)s (et) here[5]
10. des sui tota(m) p(re)d(i)c(t)am t(er)ra(m) d(i)c(t)o priori quovsq(ue) fruct(us) suos asportau(er)it (contr)*a*[6]
11. om(ne)s Warantizabu(n)t. P(re)t(er)ea p(re)dict(us) p(r)ior q(u)*a*(m)libet ac(r)*a*m d(i)c(t)e t(er)re cu(m)
12. dimidia su(m)ma auene te(m)p(or)e (com)petenti seminabit. In cui(us) rei testi[7]
13. moniu(m) huic scripto ad mod(um) Cyrog(r)*affi* (con)fecto vt(er)q(ue) illor(um) alt(er)nati(m)
14. si(n)gna sua apposueru(n)t. Hiis testib(us). Ric(ardo) capellano de pa(n)weld
15. Rog(ero) de Widekesso. Hob' le heyroun. Galfr(ido) Goding. Laure(n)[8]
16. c(i)o Machun. (et) aliis.

Translation

It is agreed between William of the Seven Mills on the one part and the Prior of 'Ging Tobie' (Thoby Priory) on the other, namely, that William has demised and granted to the said Prior and the Convent 30 acres of land, namely in the field which is called 'Lanoeland', which lie close to the highway running from Rayleigh towards London, to be sown with oats in the 36th year of the reign of Henry son of King John. And it is to be known that the said Prior will plough, sow efficiently with good oats all the aforesaid land, weed, reap and bind at his own charges. At harvest-time however the said Prior will carry away two parts of all the fruit of the said land except tithe and the said William will retain the third part. The said William and his heirs will warrant all the aforesaid land to the said Prior against all (men) until he shall have carried away his fruits. Further the aforesaid Prior will sow each acre of the said land with half the whole of the oats at the suitable time. In witness of which matter both of them have alternately set their signs to this writing composed in the form of a chirograph. These being witnesses, Richard the chaplain of 'Panweld', Roger de Widekesso, Hob' le Heyroun, Geoffrey Goding, Laurence Machun and others.

NOTE

1. The use of *v* instead of *u* initially (*see also* Plate I, n. 6). The use of *v* initially becomes more and more common and almost supplants *u* by 1400.
2. Division of word. If the meaning of a word at the end of a line is not apparent always look at the next line to see whether the word has been divided.
3. The exaggerated down stroke of letter *a* which has little or no loop, making it resemble a letter *q*.
4. The form of the *ur* sign, not an easily recognizable one in this document.
5. See Note 2.
6. The extreme abbreviation of the word *contra*.
7. See Note 2.
8. See Note 2.

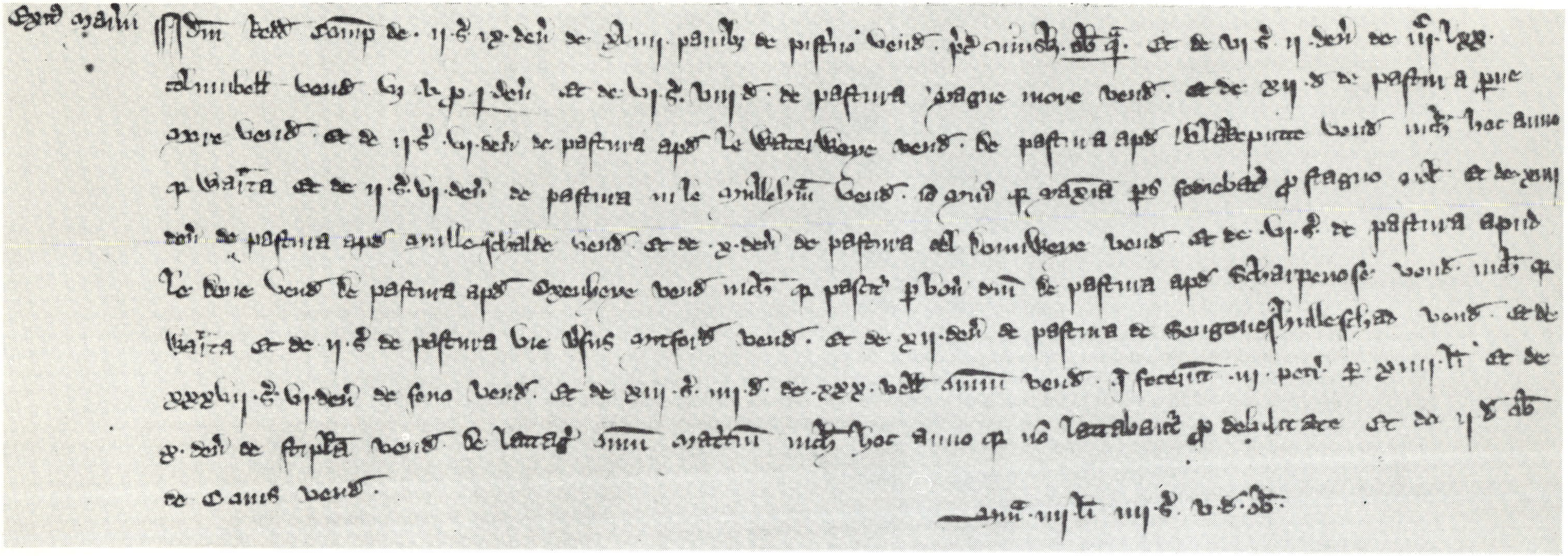

PLATE IV. BAILIFF'S ACCOUNT OF THE MANOR OF TODDENHAM, GLOUCESTERSHIRE, 1278

[Glos. R.O., D1099/M 30/1]   *Facsimile*

Exit(us) Man(er)ii (*in margin*)

1. ¹Id(e)m Redd(it) Comp(otum) de. ij. s(olidis).² ix. den(ariis) de xliiij. panib(us) de pist(r)ino vend(itis). p(re)c(io) cuiusl(ibet). ob(olo)
q(u)a(drante). Et de vj.s(olidis). ij.den(ariis) de iij.lxx.

2. columbell(is) vend(itis). v(idelicet) .v. p(ro) .j. den(ario) Et de vj. s(olidis). viij. d(enariis). de pastura Magne more vend(ita). Et de xij.
d(enariis) de pastura p(ar)ue

3. More vend(ita). Et de ij. s(olidis) .vj. den(ariis) de pastura ap(u)d le waterweye vend(ita). De pastura ap(u)d Blakeputte vend(ita) nich(il)
hoc anno

4. q(uia) war(e)cta Et de ij. s(olidis). vj. den(ariis) de pastura in le Mulleham vend(ita). i(de)o Min(us) q(uia) Maxi(m)a p(ar)s fodiebat(ur) p(ro)
stagno Mol(endini) Et de xiiij

5. den(ariis). de pastura ap(u)d Mulleschalde vend(ita). Et de .x. den(ariis de pastura del Dounweye vend(ita). Et de .vj. s(olidis). de pastura apud

6. le Dene vend(ita) De pastura ap(u)d Oxenheye vend(ita) nich(il) q(uia)) pascit(ur) p(er) bou(es) d(omi)ni De pastura ap(u)d Scharpenose
vend(ita). nich(il) q(uia)

7. war(e)cta Et de .ij. s(olidis) de pastura vie v(er)sus Mitford' vend(ita). Et de .xij. den(ariis) de pastura de Seugoueshulleschad³ vend(ita). Et de

8. xxxvij. s(olidis). vj. den(ariis) de feno vend(ito). Et de xiij .s(olidis). iiij. d(enariis). de .xxx. vell(eribus) oui(u)m⁴ vend(itis). q(ue) feceru(n)t
.iij. petr(as) p(er). xiiij. li(bras) Et de

9. x. den(ariis) de stip(u)la vend(ita). De lactag(io) ou(iu)m Mat(r)ic(u)m nich(il) hoc anno q(uia) no(n) lactabant(ur) p(ro) debilitate Et de
ij. d(enariis) ob(olo)

10. de C ouis vend(itis).

11.   S(um)ma⁵ .iiij. li(bre) .iiij. s(olidi). v. d(enarii). ob(olus).

Translation

Issues of the Manor

The same (bailiff) renders the account for 2s. 9d. from 44 loaves from the bakehouse sold at ¾d. each. And for 6s. 2d. from 370 pigeons sold, viz. 5 for 1d. And for 6s. 8d. from the pasture of Great More sold. And for 12d. from the pasture of Little More sold. And for 2s. 6d. from the pasture at the water-way sold. From the pasture at 'Blakeputte' (Black Pit) sold nothing this year because fallow. And for 2s. 6d. from the pasture in the 'Mulleham' (Mill Ham) sold, therefore less because the greatest part was dug out for the millpond. And for 14d. from the pasture at 'Mulleschalde' sold. And for 10d. from the pasture of the Down Way sold. And for 6s. from the pasture at the 'Dene' (Dean) sold. From the pasture at 'Oxenheye' (Oxney) sold nothing because it is grazed by the lord's oxen. From the pasture at 'Scharpenose' sold nothing because fallow. And for 2s. from the pasture of the way towards Mitford sold. And for 12d. from the pasture of 'Seugoueshulleschad' sold. And for 37s. 6d. from hay sold. And for 13s. 4d. from 30 fleeces sold which made 3 stones by the 14 pounds. And for 10d. from straw sold. From the milk-yield of the ewes nothing this year because they were not milked on account of weakness. And for 2½d. from 100 eggs sold.

Total 4li. 4s. 5½d.

NOTE

1. The use of the paragraph mark before *Id(e)m* like two long *ss*; these are sometimes further decorated by flourishes. The individual sections of this and similar types of record are usually indicated by a paragraph mark (see also Note 1 to Plate VI and Plate VIII). Note too that repeatedly occurring words in such documents are often subjected to extreme abbreviation.

2. The use of Þ above the line as a general sign of suspension.

3. The first two *us* could equally well be read as *ns*. See next Note.

4. As very often the strokes (minims) of letters *i*, *m*, *n* and *u* are not distinguished to indicate the individual letters intended, it may be necessary various combinations of minims, if the sense of the word is not immediately obvious from the context.

5. The exaggerated form of capital *S*, often misread as *M* by the beginner.

Already in the latter part of the 13th century the thickness and exaggeration of horizontal strokes begins to disappear and by the reign of Edward II Court Hand may often be seen in its finest form. Its main characteristics in this period are (i) an absence of the floreation and exaggeration seen in the hands of the previous century, the letters *b*, *h*, *l*, etc., being as a rule no longer split but having a simple hook curving to the right (but see some letter *h*s and *l*s in Plate V), descenders, however often tending to be rather long; (ii) the general uprightness of the writing gives a general appearance of neatness and compactness; (iii) it becomes more difficult to distinguish between *t* and *c*, as the down-stroke of *t* does not always show above the cross and the cross is started close to the down-stroke; (iv) capital *A* becomes very similar to capital *D*.

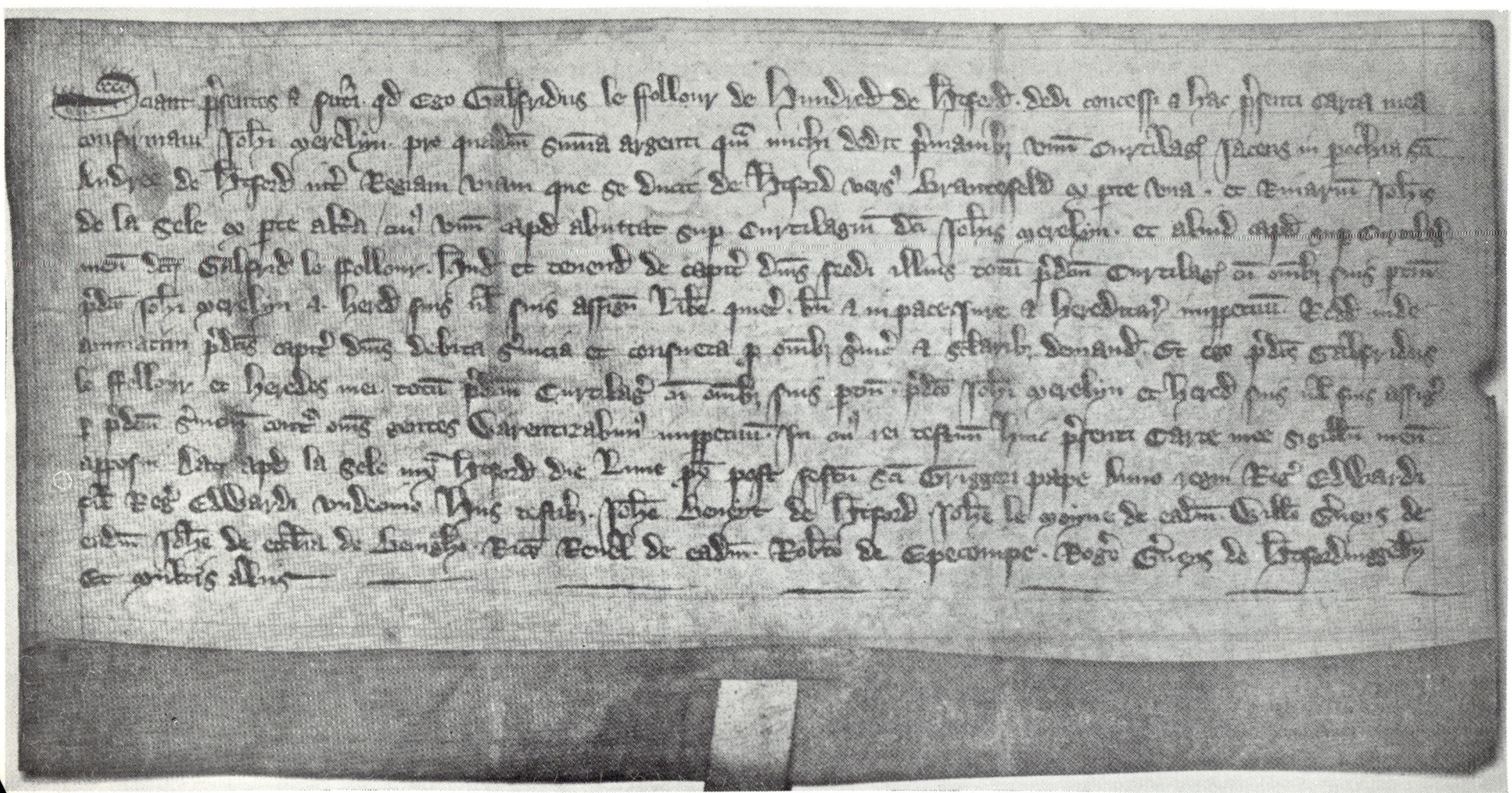

PLATE V. GRANT OF CURTILAGE IN ST. ANDREW, HERTFORD, 1318

[Herts. R.O., D/EAS 2048]

Size of original 10 in. × 4⁹/₁₀ in.

PLATE V. GRANT OF CURTILAGE IN ST. ANDREW, HERTFORD, 1318

1. Sciant[1] p(re)sentes (et) fut(ur)i[2] q(uo)d Ego Galfridus le Follour[3] de Hundred(o) de H(er)tford'. dedi concessi (et) hac p(re)senti Carta mea

2. confirmaui[4] Joh(ann)i Merelyn pro quad(a)m su(m)ma argenti q(u)am michi dedit p(re)manib(us) vnu(m) Curtilag(ium)[5] Iacens in p(ar)ochia s(an)c(t)i

3. Andree de H(er)tford' int(er) Regiam viam que se ducit de H(er)tford vers(us) Brantefeld' ex p(ar)te vna. et Riuariu(m) Joh(ann)is

4. de la Sele ex p(ar)te alt(er)a / cui(us) vnu(m) cap(u)d abuttat sup(er) Curtilagiu(m) d(i)c(t)i Joh(ann)is Merelyn. et aliud cap(u)d sup(er) Curtilag(ium)[6]

5. meu(m) d(i)ct(i) Galfrid(i) le Follour. H(abe)nd(um) et tenend(um) de capit(alibus) d(omi)nis feodi illius totu(m) p(re)d(i)c(tu)m Curtilag(ium) cu(m) o(m)nib(us) suis (per)tin(entijs)

6. p(re)d(i)c(t)o Joh(ann)i Merelyn (et). hered(ibus) suis u(e)l suis assign(atis) Lib(er)e. quiet(e). b(e)n(e). (et) in pace. Iure (et) hereditar(ie) imp(er)petuu(m). Redd(endo) inde

7. annuatim p(re)d(i)c(t)is capit(alibus) d(omi)nis debita s(er)uicia et consueta p(ro) o(m)nib(us) s(er)uic(ijs) (et) s(e)c(u)larib(us) demand(is). Et ego p(re)d(i)c(tu)s Galfridus

8. le Follour et heredes mei. totu(m) p(re)d(i)c(tu)m Curtilag(ium) cu(m) o(m)nib(us) suis p(er)tin(entijs). p(re)d(i)c(t)o Joh(ann)i Merelyn et hered(ibus) suis u(e)l suis assig(natis)

9. p(er) p(re)d(i)c(t)u(m) s(er)uiciu(m) cont(r)a om(ne)s gentes Warentizabim(us) imp(er)petuu(m). In cui(us) rei testi(moniu)m huic p(re)senti Carte mee sigillu(m) meu(m)

10. apposui Dat(a)[7] ap(u)d la Sele iux(t)a H(er)tford' die Lune p(ro)x(ima) post festu(m) s(an)c(t)i Griggori pape Anno regni Reg(is) Edwardi

11. fil(ij) Reg(is) Edwardi vndecimo. Hiis testib(us) .Joh(ann)e Beneyt de H(er)tford .Joh(ann)e le Moyne de ead(e)m. Will(elm)o G(er)ueys de

12. ead(e)m Joh(ann)e de eccl(es)ia de Beni(n)gho. Ric(ard)o Reuel de ead(e)m. Rob(er)to de Epecompe. Rog(er)o G(er)ueys de H(er)tfordinggeb(er)y

13. Et Multis aliis

Translation

Let present and future know that I Geoffrey le Follour of the Hundred of Hertford have given, granted and by this my present charter have confirmed to John Merelyn, for a certain sum of silver which he gave to me beforehand, one curtilage lying in the parish of St. Andrew of Hertford between the highway which leads from Hertford towards Bramfield on the one part and the river-bank of John de la Sele on the other part, whereof one head abuts upon the curtilage of the said John Merelyn and the other head upon the curtilage of me, the said Geoffrey le Follour, to have and to hold of the chief lords of that fee all the aforesaid curtilage with all its appurtenances to the aforesaid John Merelyn and his heirs or his assigns freely, quietly, well and in peace, by right and inheritance for ever, paying therefor annually to the aforesaid chief lords the due services and customs for all services and secular demands. And I the aforesaid Geoffrey le Follour and my heirs will warrant all the aforesaid curtilage with all its appurtenances to the aforesaid John Merelyn and his heirs or his assigns by the aforesaid service against all people for ever. In witness of which thing I have set my seal to this my present charter. Given at 'la Sele' near to Hertford on Monday next after the Feast of St. Gregory the Pope in the eleventh year of the reign of King Edward son of King Edward. These being witnesses, John Beneyt of Hertford, John le Moyne of the same, William Gerveys of the same, John of the church of Bengeo, Richard Revel of the same, Robert of Epecompe, Roger Gerveys of Hertingfordbury, and many others.

NOTE

1. Exaggerated forms of *S* are still being used.
2. The form of the *ur* sign.
3. That *ff* = *F* and should never be transcribed *Ff*.
4. A dash instead of a dot above the letter *i* is common at this time. When *i* is the last letter of a word the dash is sometimes written currently from it and can be mistaken for a sign of abbreviation.
5. The use of ꝑ sign as a general sign of suspension.
6. The use of ꝺ sign as a general sign of suspension.
7. The similarity of *D* in *Dat(a)* and *A* in *Anno* (on the same line).

The generally high standard of calligraphy in the first quarter of the 14th century tends not to be maintained, though well-written hands are by no means unknown thereafter. Writing at first became rounder (Plate VI) and later rather more angular (Plate VII). If anything, the letters *i*, *m*, *n* and *u* become yet more difficult to distinguish; and the closed *e* often mistaken for *o* comes into use. Some forms of capitals *C*, *E* and *O* have similarities which may lead to misreading.

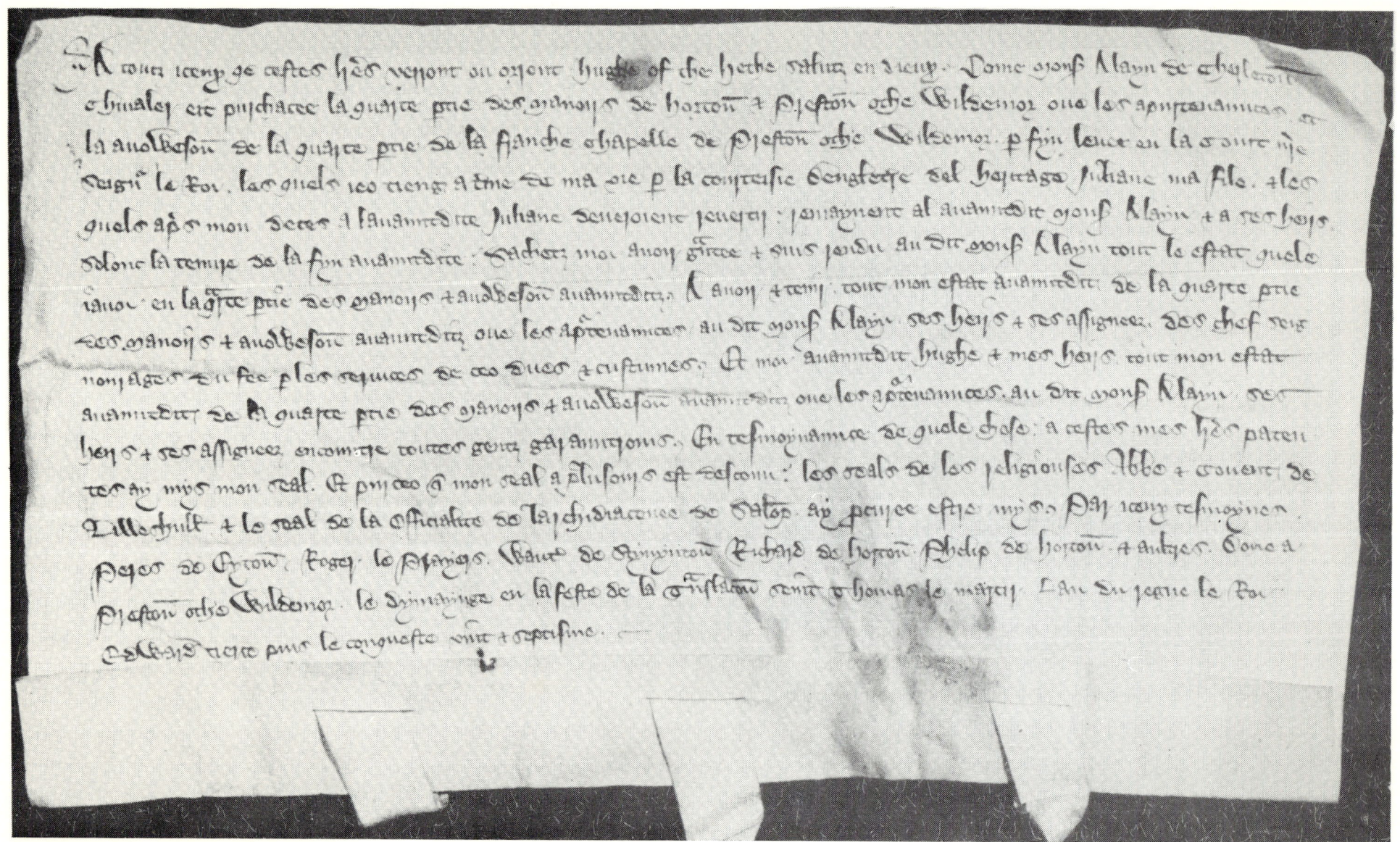

PLATE VI. RELEASE OF FOURTH PART OF TWO MANORS AND A FREE CHAPEL, NORTHAMPTONSHIRE, 1353

[Northants. R.O., Knightley Charter 92]

Size of original 9½ in. × 5½ in.

1. [1]A toutz iceux qe cestes l(ett)res verront[2] ou orront Hughe of the Hethe salutz en dieux)·Come Mons(ire) Alayn de Cherleton'[3]
2. Chiualer eit purchacee la quarte p(ar)tie des Manoirs de Horton' (et) Preston' othe Wildemor oue les apurtenaunces et
3. la auoweso(u)n de la quarte p(ar)tie de la franche chapelle de Preston' othe Wildemor. p(ar) fyn leuee en la Court n(ost)re
4. Seign(ur) le Roi. les quels ieo tiens a t(er)me de ma vie p(ar) la courteisie Denglet(er)re del heritage Juliane ma file . (et) les
5. quels ap(re)s mon deces a lauauntdite Juliane deueroient reuertir؛ remaynent al auauntdit Mons(ire) Alayn (et) a ses heirs
6. solonc la tenure de la fyn auauntdite؛ Sachetz moi auoir g(r)antee (et) suis rendu au dit Mons(ire) Alayn tout le estat quele
7. iauoi en la q(u)arte p(ar)tie des Manoirs (et) auoweso(u)n auauntditz) A auoir (et) tenir tout mon estat auauntdit de la quarte p(ar)tie
8. des Manoirs (et) auoweso(u)n auauntditz oue les ap(ur)tenaunces au dit Mons(ire) Alayn ses heirs (et) ses assigneez. des chef seig[4]
9. nourages du fee p(ar) les seruices de ceo dues (et) custumes) Et moi auauntdit Hughe (et) mes heirs tout mon estat
10. auauntdit de la quarte p(ar)tie des Manoirs (et) auoweso(u)n auauntditz oue les ap(ur)tenaunces. au dit Mons(ire) Alayn ses
11. heirs (et) ses assigneez encountre toutes gentz garauntroms) En tesmoynaunce de quele chose؛ a ceste mes l(ett)res paten[5]
12. tes ay mys mon seal. Et purceo q(e) mon seal a plusours est desconu؛ les seals de les religiouses Abbe (et) Couent de
13. Lilleshull' (et) le seal de la Officialite de larchidiaconee de Salop'. ay p(ro)curee estre mys. Par iceux tesmoynes
14. Peres de Eyton' ⟨ Roger le Prayers. Waut(er) de Styuynton'. Richard de Horton'. Phelip de Horton'. (et) aultres. Done a
15. Preston' othe Wildemor. le dymaynge en la feste de la T(r)anslac(i)on seint Thomas le martir. Lan du regne le Roi
16. Edward tierce puis le conqueste vint (et) septisme.

Translation

To all those who will see or hear these letters Hugh of the Hethe sends greeting in God. Whereas Sir Alayn de Cherleton knight has purchased the fourth part of the Manors of Horton and Preston-on-the-Wild-Moor with the appurtenances and the advowson of the fourth part of the free chapel of Preston-on-the-Wild-Moor by fine levied in the Court of our lord King, which I hold for the term of my life by the courtesy of England of the inheritance of Juliana, my daughter, and which after my decease ought to revert to the aforesaid Juliana, remainder to the aforesaid Sir Alayn and to his heirs according to the tenor of the fine aforesaid, know that I have granted and surrendered to the said Sir Alayn all the estate which I had in the fourth part of the manors and advowson aforesaid, to have and to hold all my estate aforesaid of the fourth part of the manors and advowson aforesaid with the appurtenances to the said Sir Alayn his heirs and his assigns of the chief lordships of the fee by the services therefor due and accustomed. And I the aforesaid Hugh and my heirs will warrant all my estate aforesaid of the fourth part of the manors and advowson aforesaid with the appurtenances to the said Sir Alayn, his heirs and assigns against all people. In witness of which thing I have put to these my letters patent my seal, and because my seal is unknown to many, I have procured to be put the seals of the men of religion, the Abbot and Convent of Lilleshall and the seal of the Official of the Archdeaconry of Shropshire, by these witnesses Peter of Eyton, Roger le Prayers, Walter of Styvynton, Richard of Horton, Philip of Horton and others. Given at Preston-on-the-Wild-Moor on Sunday on the Feast of the Translation of Saint Thomas the Martyr in the twenty-seventh year of the reign of King Edward the third after the Conquest.

NOTE

1. The flourished paragraph mark before the first letter. Although resembling a superior *a* it probably developed out of a hurriedly written capital *C* (for *Capitulum*).
2. The two forms of *r* used in this single word. The first derives from the ligature of *or* and was used in the 11th and 12th centuries only after *o*. In the next century it is written increasingly after other rounded letters such as *b*, *d* or *p*. In the 14th century it is found after other bowed letters, but it will be noticed that in this charter it is still only written after *o*. In the 15th century, it is used with any letters. Before the 14th century it generally in resembles an Arabic figure 2; the addition of a tail at its base in hands of that century, as seen here, makes it sometimes liable to confusion with the abbreviation sign for *us* or *et* or letter *z*. The other form is the contemporary rendering of the minuscule *r*.
3. The sign of contraction above the *n* of *Cherleton'*. It became common to put such signs after the final consonants of English words and even medially in the case of *h*, even though no extension appears possible and was probably not intended by the scribe, being merely a survival from the abbreviation of latin words.
4. Division of word.
5. Division of word.

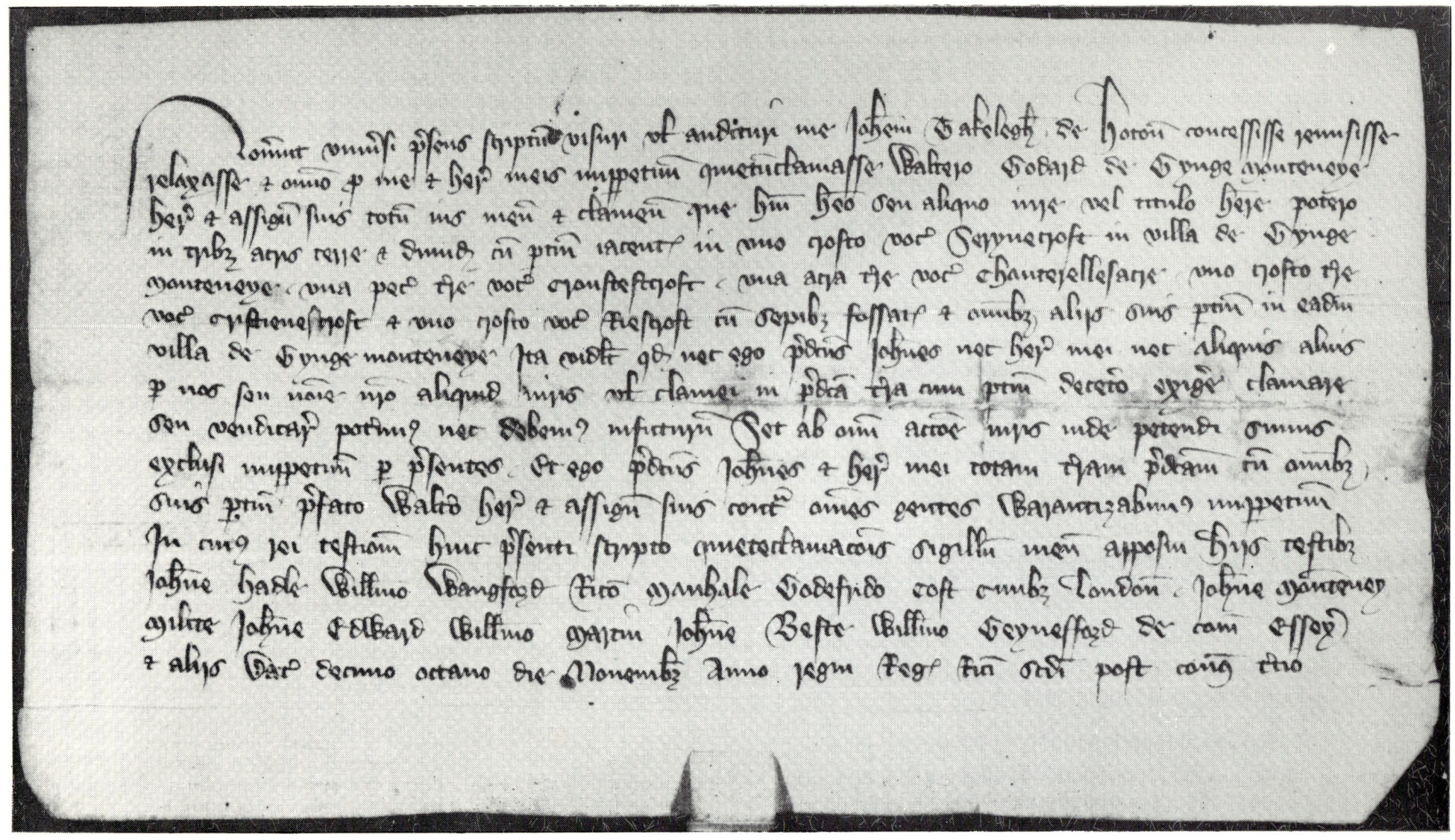

PLATE VII. QUITCLAIM OF LAND IN MOUNTNESSING, ESSEX, 1379

[Essex R.O., D/DP T1/250]

Facsimile

PLATE VII. QUITCLAIM OF LAND IN MOUNTNESSING, ESSEX, 1379

1. Nou(er)int[1] vniu(er)si p(re)sens scriptu(m) visuri v(e)l audituri[2] me Joh(ann)em Takelegh' de Hoton' concessisse remisisse
2. relaxasse (et) om(n)i(n)o p(ro) me (et) her(edibus) meis imp(er)petuu(m) quietu(m)clamasse Waltero Godard de Gynge Monteneye
3. her(edibus) (et) assign(atis) suis totu(m) ius meu(m) (et) clameu(m) que h(ab)ui h(ab)eo seu aliquo iure vel titulo h(ab)ere potero
4. in trib(us) acris terre (et) dimid(ia) cu(m) p(er)tin(encijs) iacent(ibus) in vno crofto voc(ato) Serynecroft in villa de Gynge
5. Monteneye / vna pec(ia) t(er)re voc(ata) Croustestcroft / vna acra t(er)re voc(ata) Chanterellesacre / vno crofto t(er)re
6. voc(ato) Christienescroft (et) vno crofto voc(ato) Riescroft cu(m) sepib(us) fossat(is) (et) om(n)ib(us) alijs suis p(er)tin(encijs) in ead(e)m
7. villa de Gynge monteneye Ita vid(e)l(ice)t q(uo)d[3] nec ego p(re)d(i)c(t)us Joh(an)nes nec[4] her(edes) mei nec aliquis alius
8. p(er) nos seu no(m)i(n)e n(ost)ro aliquid iuris v(e)l clamei in p(re)d(i)c(t)a t(er)ra cum p(er)tin(encijs) decet(er)o exig(er)e clamare
9. seu vendicar(e) pot(er)im(us) nec debem(us) infuturu(m) Set ab om(n)i acc(i)o(n)e iuris inde petend(i) simus
10. exclusi imp(er)petuu(m) p(er) p(re)sentes/.Et ego p(re)d(i)c(t)us Joh(an)nes (et) her(edes) mei totam t(er)ram p(re)d(i)c(t)am cu(m) om(n)ib(us)
11. suis p(er)tin(encijs) p(re)fato Walt(er)o her(edibus) (et) assign(atis) suis cont(r)a om(n)es gentes warantizabim(us) imp(er)petuu(m)
12. In cui(us) rei testi(m)o(niu)m huic p(re)senti scripto quieteclamac(i)o(n)is sigillu(m) meu(m) apposui Hijs testib(us)
13. Joh(an)ne Hadle Will(el)mo Wangford' Ric(ard)o Manhale Godefrido Cost Ciuib(us) London' Joh(an)ne Mou(n)teney
14. Milite Joh(an)ne Edward Will(el)mo Martin[5] Joh(an)ne Beste Will(el)mo Geynesford de com(itatu) Essex(ie)
15. (et) alijs Dat' decimo octauo die Nouemb(ris) Anno regni Reg(is) Ric(ard)i s(e)c(un)di post conq(uestum) t(er)cio

Translation

Be it known to all men who will see or hear the present writing that I, John Takelegh of Hutton, have granted, remised released and completely for me and my heirs for ever quitclaimed to Walter Godard of Mountnessing, his heirs and assigns all my right and claim which I had, have or by any right or title will be able to have in three acres of land and a half with the appurtenances lying in a croft called 'Serynecroft' in the township of Mountnessing, one piece of land called 'Croustestcroft', one acre of land called 'Chanterellesacre', one croft of land called 'Christienescroft' and one croft called 'Riescroft' with the hedges, ditches and all other their appurtenances in the same township of Mountnessing, namely, so that neither I the aforesaid John nor my heirs nor anyone else by us or in our name will be able or ought henceforth to demand, claim or pretend to anything of right or claim in the aforesaid land with the appurtenances in the future, but we are to be excluded from pleading all action of law thereof for ever by the presents. And I, the aforesaid John, and my heirs will warrant all the land aforesaid with all its appurtenances to the aforementioned Walter, his heirs and assigns against all people for ever. In witness of which matter I have set to this present writing of quitclaim my seal. These being witnesses, John Hadle, William Wangford, Richard Manhale, Godfrey Cost, citizens of London, John Mounteney, knight, John Edward, William Martin, John Beste, William Geynesford of the county of Essex and others. Given the eighteenth day of November in the third year of the reign of King Richard the second after the Conquest.

NOTE

1. The exaggerated form of capital *N*.
2. Letter *i* may or may not be dotted or accented. If accented, as in the last letter of *audituri*, the accent is easily mistaken for a sign of abbreviation or contraction.
3. The contraction of *quod* is indicated by a flourish continuing from the final stroke of letter *d*. This becomes the common form.
4. How a badly written *e* could easily be mistaken for *o*.
5. See Note 2.

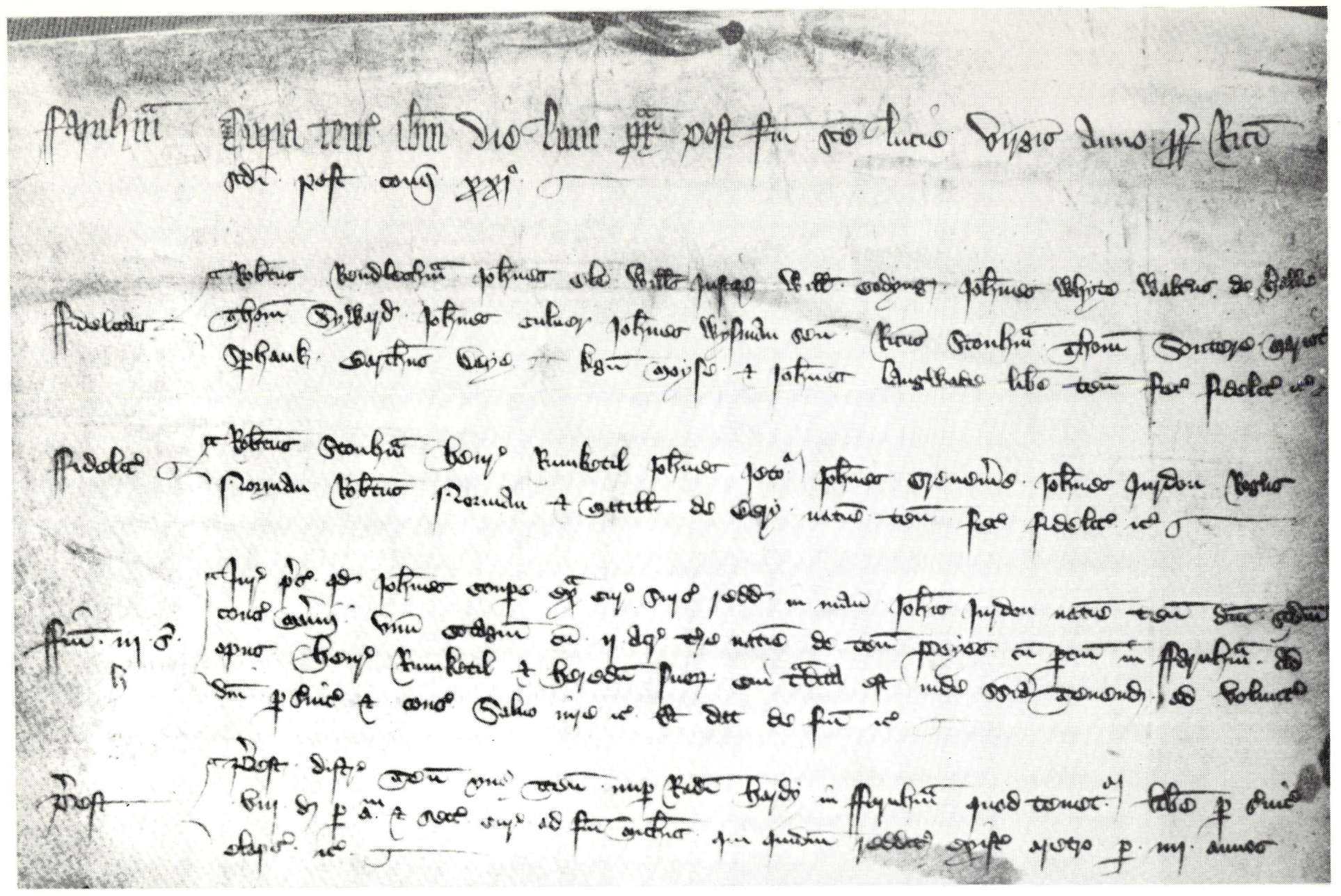

PLATE VIII. COURT ROLL OF THE MANOR OF FARNHAM, SUFFOLK, 1397

[Essex R.O., D/DRg 1/56]

Facsimile

PLATE VIII   COURT ROLL OF THE MANOR OF FARNHAM, SUFFOLK, 1397

1. Farnh*a*m	Curia[1] tent(a) ib(ide)m die Lune p(ro)x(im)*a* Post f(estu)m s(an)c(t)e Lucie virg(in)is Anno r(egni) r(egis) Ric(ard)i
2.	s(e)c(un)di post conq(uestum) xxj⁰
3.	Rob(er)tus Rendlesh*a*m[2] Joh(an)nes Ole Will(elmus) Justize Will(elmus) Godyng' Joh(an)nes Whyte Walt(er)us de Helle
4. Fidelitas	Thom(as) Syward Joh(an)nes Culuer Joh(an)nes Wysman sen(ior) Ric(ard)us Stonh*a*m Thom(as) Soutere Mariot'
5.	Sp(ar)hauk Barth(olome)us Deye — Agn(es) Moyse (et) Joh(an)nes Langwade lib(er)e ten(entes) fec(erunt) fidelit(atem) (et)c'
6. Fidelitas	Rob(er)tus Stonh*a*m Henr(icus) Rumketil Joh(an)nes Jeto(ur)[3] Joh(an)nes Grenem(er)e. Joh(an)nes Jurdon Rog(er)us
7.	Norman Rob(er)tus Norman (et) Matill(da) de Bery nati(u)e ten(entes) fec(erunt) fidelit(atem) (et)c'
8.	Jur(ati) p(re)s(entant)[4]. q(uo)d Joh(an)nes Coup(er)e ex(tr)a Cur(iam) Surs(um) redd(idit) in man(u) Joh(ann)is Jurdon nati(u)e ten(entis) d(omi)ni .s(e)c(un)d(u)m
9.	cons(uetudinem) Man(er)ij. vnu(m) Cotagiu(m) cu(m) .ij. acr(is) t(er)re nati(u)e de ten(emento) Peyes. cu(m) p(er)tin(entijs) in Farnh*a*m . ad
10. Fin(is) .iij.s'.	opus Henr(ici) Rumketil (et) heredu(m) suor(um) Cui t(r)*a*dita est inde s(ei)si(n)a Tenend(um) ad volunt(atem)
11. H[5]	d(omi)ni p(er) s(er)uic(ium) (et) cons(uetudinem). Saluo iure (et)c' Et dat de fin(e) (et)c'.
12.	P(receptum)[6] est distr(ingere) Ten(entem) vni(us) Ten(ementi). nup(er) Rad(ulph)i Hardy in Farnh*a*m quod tenet(ur). lib(er)e p(er) s(er)uic(ium)
13. P(receptum)est	.viij. d' p(er) a(nnu)*m* (et) sect(e) Cur(ie) ad f(estu)m Mich(el)is qui quid(e)m reddit(us) exist(it) aretro p(er) .iiij. annos
14.	elaps(os). (et)c'

Translation

Farnham	Court held there on Monday next after the Feast of St. Lucy the Virgin in the 21st year of the reign of King Richard the second after the Conquest.
Fealty	Robert Rendlesham, John Ole, William Justize, William Godyng, John Whyte, Walter de Helle, Thomas Syward, John Culver, John Wysman the elder, Richard Stonham, Thomas Soutere, Mariot Sparhauk, Bartholomew Deye, Agnes Moyse and John Langwade, free tenants, have made fealty, etc.
Fealty	Robert Stonham, Henry Rumketil, John Jetour, John Grenemere, John Jurdon, Roger Norman, Robert Norman and Matilda de Bery, bond tenants, have made fealty, etc.
Fine 3s. H	The jurors present that John Coupere out of court has surrendered into the hand of John Jurdon, bond tenant of the lord, according to the custom of the manor, one cottage with 2 acres of bond land belonging to Peyes tenement with the appurtenances in Farnham to the use of Henry Rumketil and his heirs, to whom seisin thereof was delivered, to hold at the will of the lord by service and custom, saving the right, etc. And he gives as fine, etc.
Order	Order is made to distrain the tenant of a tenement formerly of Ralph Hardy in Farnham, which is held freely by service of 8d. yearly and suit of court at the Feast of Michael, which same rent has been in arrears for 4 years past, etc.

NOTE

1. Treatment of capital *C* by the scribe. See also Note 1 to Plate X.
2. See Note 5 to Plate II.
3. The flourished form of the sign for *ur* giving little indication that it springs from the round *r*.
4. An example of extreme abbreviation of a word frequently used in such a record.
5. Added by a later hand; possibly signifying that the holding owed a heriot as a tenurial obligation.
6. See Note 4.

The tendency towards angularity seen in the latter part of the previous century becomes further developed and these scripts are often of a high standard during the reign of Henry VI, though much cruder less angular and formal hands are also to be found in local records (Plate IX). These crude, even ugly hands, become very common in the closing decades of this century. In all these scripts the minims of *i*, *m*, *n* and *u* remain difficult to differentiate, the dotting or accenting of *i* being only haphazardly done, if at all. The letters *b* and *v* may have very similar forms and are therefore liable to confusion (see Plate X). The development of the 'upside down' form of *e* is also to be noted.

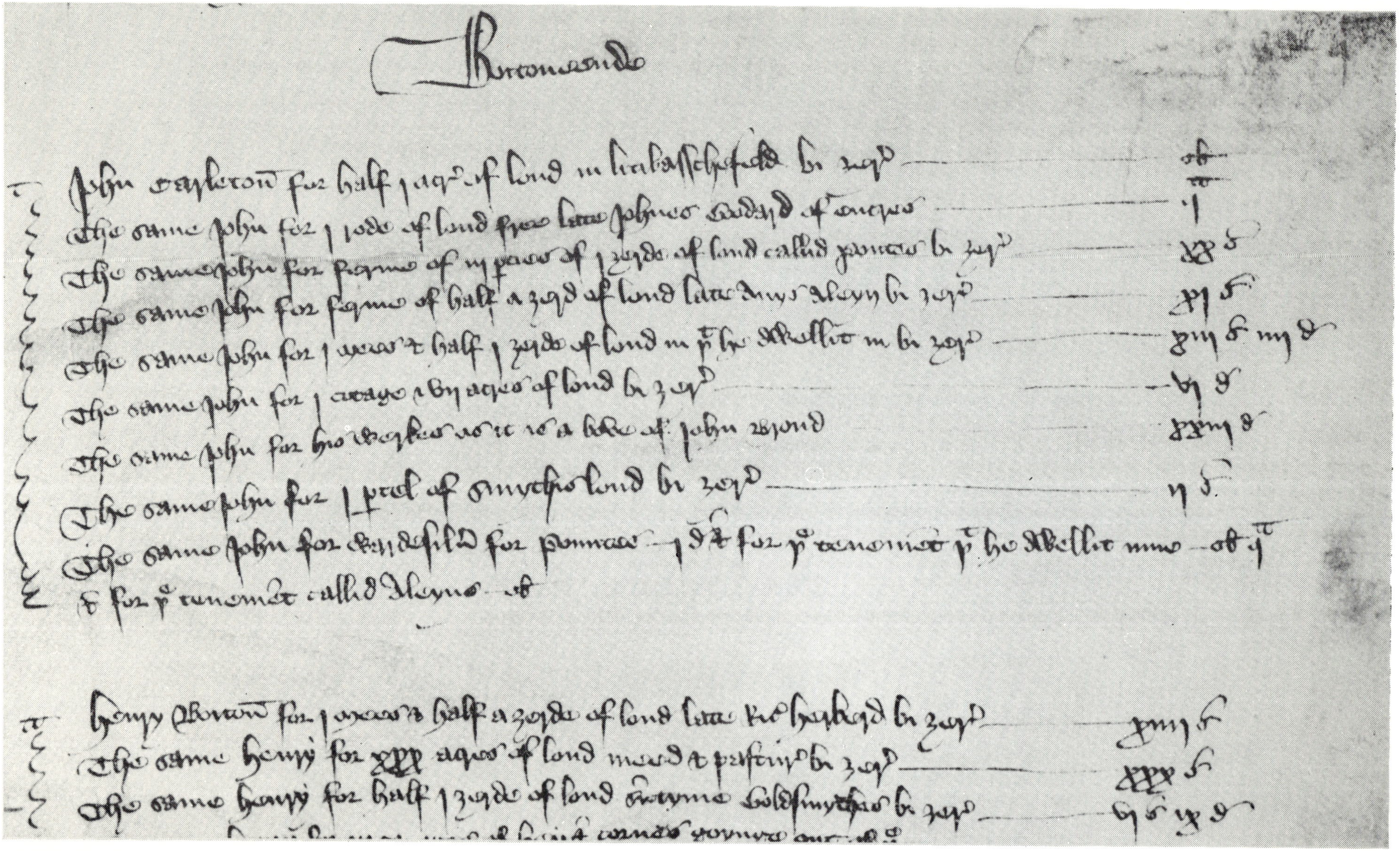

PLATE IX. RENTAL OF THE MANOR AND BOROUGH OF THAXTED, 1416

[Essex R.O., D/DHu M19]

Facsimile

PLATE IX. RENTAL OF THE MANOR AND BOROUGH OF THAXTED, 1416

1.   Boitoneende
2. John Carleton' for half j acr(e)[1] of lond in litilasschefeld bi yer(e)[2] .. .. ob'[3]
3. The same John for j rode of lond free late Johnes Goodard of encres .. .. q^{a}[4]
4. The same John for ferme of iij p(ar)ties of j yerde of lond[5] callid Pontes bi yer(e) .. .. xxs'
5. The same John for ferme of half a yerd of lond late Auys Aleyn bi yer(e) .. .. xjs'
6. The same John for j Mees[6] (and) half j yerde of lond in (tha)t[7] he dwellit in bi yer(e) .. .. xiijs' iiijd'
7. The same John for j cotage (and) vij acres of lond bi yer(e) .. .. vjd'
8. The same John for his werkes as it is a bove of John Brond .. .. xxiijd'
9. The same John for j p(ar)cel of Smythislond bi yer(e) .. .. ijs'
10. The same John for wardesilu(er) for Pounces – jd' (and) for (th)e teneme(n)t (tha)t he dwellit inne – ob'q^{a}
11. (and) for (th)e teneme(n)t callid Aleyns – ob'

12. Henry Boiton' for j Mees (and) half a yerde of lond late Ric(hard) Herberd bi yer(e) .. .. xiiijs'
13. The same Henry for xxx acres of lond meed (and) pastur(e) bi yer(e) .. .. xxxs'
14. The same Henry for half j yerde of lond su(m)tyme Goldsmythes bi yer(e) .. .. vjs' ixd'[8]

NOTE

1. The common suspension sign for the Latin *acra* in all cases is here carried over into English. This is commonly used after *r* – see yer(e) at the end of the line.
2. The z-like 'yogh' (see Table of Signs and p.2), printed here as a *y*.
3. I.e. *ob(olus)*, Latin for halfpenny.
4. I.e. *q(u)a(drans)*, Latin for farthing.
5. Yardland or virgate (of varying extent by custom, but commonly 30 acres, i.e. ¼ hide).
6. Mees = messuage.
7. Use of 'thorn' (see Table of Signs and p.2), printed here as *th*.
8. It is uncommon to find such a record written in English at this date.

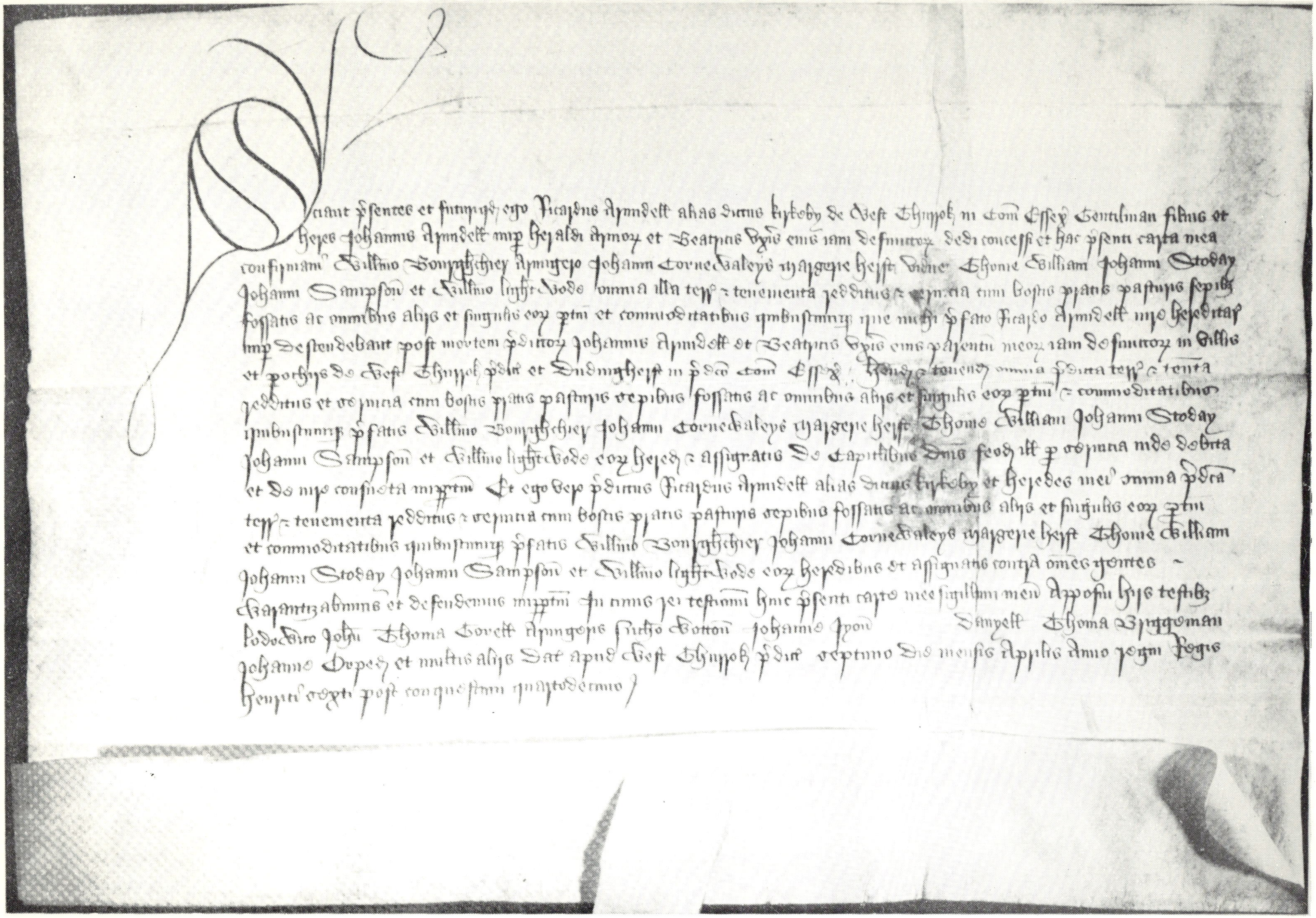

PLATE X. GRANT OF AN ESTATE IN WEST THURROCK AND DODDINGHURST, 1436
[Essex R.O., D/DP T1/259]

Size of original 10¼ in. × 7 in.

PLATE X. GRANT OF AN ESTATE IN WEST THURROCK AND DODDINGHURST, 1436

1. Sciant[1] p(re)sentes[2] et futuri q(uo)d ego Ricardus Arundell'[3] alias dictus Kirkeby de West Thurrok' in Com(itatu) Essex' Gentilman filius et
2. heres Johannis Arundell' nup(er) heraldi armor(um) et Beatricis vx(or)is eius iam defunctor(um) dedi concessi et hac p(re)senti carta mea
3. confirmaui Will(el)mo Bourgh'chier[4] armigero Johanni Cornewaleys Margerie Herst vidue Thome William Johanni Stoday
4. Johanni Sampson' et Will(el)mo Ligh'twode omnia illa terr(as) (et) tenementa redditus (et) seruicia cum boscis pratis pasturis sepib(us)
5. fossatis ac omnibus alijs et singulis eor(um) p(er)tin(entijs) et commoditatibus quibuscumq(ue) que michi p(re)fato Ricardo Arundell' iure hereditar(io)
6. nup(er) descendebant post mortem p(re)dictor(um) Johannis Arundell' et Beatricis vx(or)is eius parentu(m) meor(um) iam defunctor(um) in villis
7. et p(ar)ochijs de West Thurrok' p(re)dict' et Dudingherst in p(re)d(i)c(t)o Com(itatu) Essex' H(ab)end(um) (et) tenend(um) omnia p(re)dicta terr(as) (et) ten(emen)ta
8. redditus et seruicia cum boscis pratis pasturis sepibus fossatis ac omnibus alijs et singulis eor(um) p(er)tin(entijs) (et) commoditatibus
9. quibuscumq(ue) p(re)fatis Will(elm)o Bourgh'chier Johanni Cornewaleys Margerie Herst Thome William Johanni Stoday
10. Johanni Sampson' et Will(el)mo Ligh'twode eor(um) hered(ibus) (et) assignatis De Capit(a)libus D(omi)nis feod(i) ill(ius) p(er) seruicia inde debita
11. et de iure consueta imp(er)p(e)t(uu)m Et ego vero p(re)dictus Ricardus Arundell' alias dictus Kirkeby et heredes mei omnia p(re)d(i)c(t)a
12. terr(as) (et) tenementa redditus (et) seruicia cum boscis pratis pasturis sepibus fossatis ac omnibus alijs et singulis eor(um) p(er)tin(entijs)
13. et commoditatibus quibuscumq(ue) p(re)fatis Will(el)mo Bourgh'chier Johanni Cornewaleys Margerie Herst Thome William
14. Johanni Stoday Johanni Sampson' et Will(el)mo Ligh'twode eor(um) heredibus et assignatis contra om(n)es gentes –
15. warrantizabimus et defendemus imp(er)p(e)t(uu)m In cuius rei testi(m)o(n)i(u)m huic p(re)senti carte mee sigillum meu(m) Apposui Hijs testib(us)
16. Lodowico Joh'n Thoma Torell'[5] Armigeris Nich(ola)o Wotton' Johanne Iyon' (blank) Danyell' Thoma Briggeman
17. Johanne Orped' et multis alijs Dat(a) apud West Thurrok' p(re)dict' septimo Die mensis Aprilis Anno regni Regis
18. Henrici sexti post conquestum quartodecimo/

Translation

Be it known to present and future that I, Richard Arundell otherwise called Kirkeby of West Thurrock in the County of Essex, 'gentilman', son and heir of John Arundell, formerly herald of arms, and Beatrice, his wife, now deceased, have given, granted and by this my present charter confirmed to William Bourghchier, esquire, John Cornewaleys, Margery Herst, widow, Thomas William, John Stoday, John Sampson and William Lightwode, all those lands and tenements, rents and services with the woods, meadows, pastures, hedges, ditches and all other and singular their appurtenances and commodities whatsoever which formerly descended to me the aforementioned Richard Arundell by hereditary right after the death of the aforesaid John Arundell and Beatrice, his wife, my parents now deceased, in the townships and parishes of West Thurrock aforesaid and Doddinghurst in the aforesaid County of Essex, to have and to hold all the aforesaid lands and tenements, rents and services with the woods, meadows, pastures, hedges, ditches and all other and singular their appurtenances and commodities whatsoever to the aforementioned William Bourghchier, John Cornewaleys, Margery Herst, Thomas William, John Stoday, John Sampson and William Lightwode, their heirs and assigns, of the chief lords of the fee by the services thereof due and of right accustomed for ever. And surely I, the aforesaid Richard Arundell otherwise called Kirkeby, and my heirs will warrant and defend all the aforesaid lands and tenements, rents and services, with the woods, meadows, pastures, hedges, ditches and all other and singular their appurtenances and commodities whatsoever to the aforementioned William Bourghchier, John Cornewaleys, Margery Herst, Thomas William, John Stoday, John Sampson and William Lightwode, their heirs and assigns against all people for ever. In witness of which thing I have set my seal to this my present charter. These being witnesses, Lewis John, Thomas Torell, esquires, Nicholas Wotton, John Iyon, (blank) Danyell, Thomas Briggeman, John Orped and many others. Given at West Thurrock aforesaid on the seventh day of April in the fourteenth year of the reign of King Henry the sixth after the Conquest.

NOTE

1. Elaborate form of *S*. Initial letters may receive highly individualistic treatment from a scribe.
2. Note the two forms of *e* used, e.g., in *p(re)sentes* and in *Kirkeby*; the latter form if badly written can easily be confused with *o*.
3. See note 3 to Plate VI.
4. See Note 3 to Plate VI.
5. A long *r* is used throughout the document, except in this name and in *Orped'* (l.17).

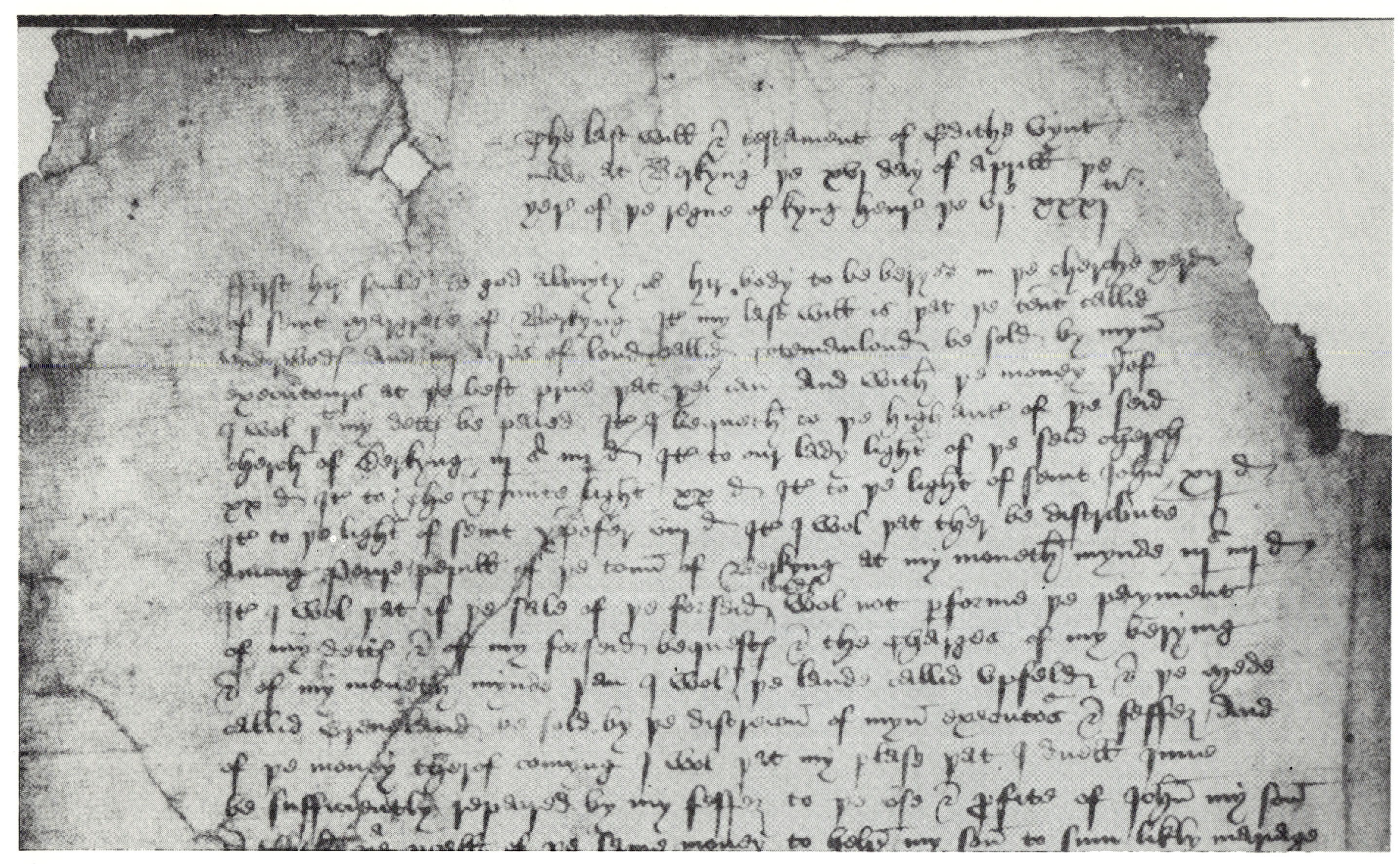

PLATE XI. CONTEMPORARY COPY OF WILL OF EDITH VYNT OF BARKING, ESSEX, 1453

[Essex R.O., D/AEW 1/178]

Facsimile

PLATE XI. CONTEMPORARY COPY OF WILL OF EDITH VYNT OF BARKING, ESSEX, 1453

1.   The last will'[1] (and)[2] testament of Edithe Vynt
2.   made at Berkyng (th)e[3] xvj day of Aprill' (th)e
3.   yer' of (th)e regne of Kyng Henr' (th)e vj^e xxxj^{tl}
4. First hir soule to god almyty (et)c' hir body to be beryed in (th)e cherche yerd'
5. of seint Margrete of Berkyng It(em) my last will' is (th)at (th)e ten(emen)t callid
6. vndirwod(es) And iiij acres of lond callid Cotemanlond be sold by myn'
7. executours at (th)e best price (th)at (th)ei can And with' (th)e money (ther)of
8. I wol (tha)t my dett(es) be paied It(em) I bequeth' to (th)e high aut(er) of (th)e seid
9. cherch' of Berkyng iijs' iiij d' It(em) to our lady ligh't[4] of (th)e seid cherch'
10. xx d' It(em) to The Trinite ligh't xx d' It(em) to (th)e ligh't of seint Joh'n xij d'
11. It(em) to (th)e ligh't of seint (Christ)ofer[5] viij d' It(em) I wol (th)at ther be distribute
12. among Poure pepill' of (th)e toun' of Berkyng at my moneth' mynde[6] iijs' iiij d'
13. It(em) I wol (th)at if (th)e sale of (th)e forseid (lond' *interlined*) wol not p(er)forme (th)e payment
14. of my dett(es) (and) of my forseid bequest(es) (and) the Charges of my berying
15. (and) of my moneth' mynde (th)an I wol ((tha)t *interlined*) (th)e lande callid vpfeld' (and) (th)e Mede
16. callid Greneland' be sold by (th)e discrec(i)on of myn' executo(ur)s (and) feffez / And
17. of (th)e money therof comyng I wol (th)at my plase (th)at I duell' Inne
18. be sufficiently repaired by my feffez to (th)e vse (and) p(ro)fite of Joh'n my son'

NOTE

1. It will be seen that final consonants *ll*, *n*, *r* and *d* on occasion, and letter *h* both medially and finally consistently, bear apparent marks of abbreviation. In documents written in English it is difficult to determine whether suspension or contraction are really intended or whether they represent habit in a scribe accustomed to writing in Latin, or even doubt in his mind as to spelling. In the absence of other confirmatory evidence, it is preferable not to attempt extension but to reproduce the flourishes by apostrophes.
2. The Tironian sign for *et* is carried over into English to represent *and*.
3. The consistent use of 'thorn' (see Note 7 to Plate IX).
4. See Note 1 above. Here clearly the scribe could not have intended to indicate a contraction by the line through the ascender of *h* in *light*; whereas in *John* (l. 10) the modified *h* may be regarded perhaps as carrying over into English the common contraction of *Johannes* (Joh'nes).
5. See Note 1 to Plate XII.
6. 'Moneth mynde' means the commemoration of a deceased person by the celebration of masses on the day one month after the date of his or her death.

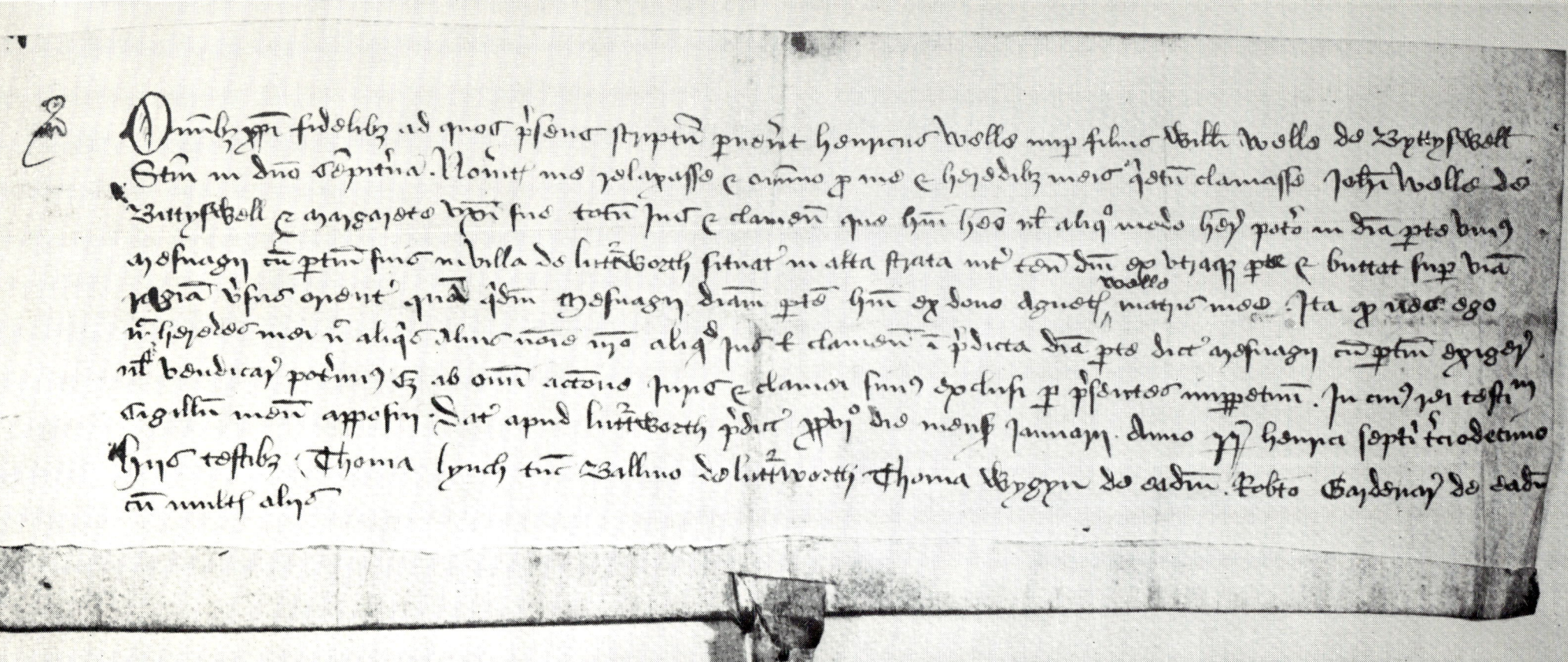

PLATE XII. QUITCLAIM OF MOIETY OF A MESSUAGE IN LUTTERWORTH, LEICESTERSHIRE, 1498

[Coventry City R.O.]

Size of original 12¾ in. × 4¾ in.

1. Om(n)ib(us) (Christ)i[1] fidelib(us) ad quos p(re)sens scriptu(m) p(er)uen(er)it henricus Welle nup(er) filius Will(elm)i Welle de Byttyswell'

2. S(alu)t(e)m[2] in d(omi)no se(m)pit(er)na(m). Nou(er)it(is) me relaxasse (et) om(n)ino p(ro) me (et) heredib(us) meis q(u)ietu(m) clamasse Joh(ann)i Welle de

3. Bittyswell (et) Margarete vx(or)i sue totu(m) Jus (et) clameu(m) que h(ab)ui h(ab)eo u(e)l aliq(u)o modo h(ab)er(e) pot(er)o in di(midi)a p(ar)te vni(us)

4. Mesuagij cu(m) p(er)tin(entijs) suis in villa de lutt(ur)worth situat(i) in alta strata int(er) ten(ementa) d(omi)ni ex vtraq(ue) p(ar)te (et) buttat sup(er) via(m)

5. regia(m) v(er)sus orient(em) qua(m) q(u)id(e)m Mesuagij di(midi)am p(ar)te(m) h(ab)ui ex dono Agnet(is) Welle matris mee. Ita q(uod) nec ego

6. n(e)c heredes mei n(e)c aliq(u)is alius no(m)i(n)e n(ost)ro aliq(uo)d Jus (ve)l[3] clameu(m) i(n) p(re)dicta di(midi)a p(ar)te dict(i) Mesuagij cu(m) p(er)tin(entijs) exiger(e)

7. u(e)l[4] vendicar(e) pot(er)im(us) s(et) ab om(n)i act(i)one Juris (et) clamei sim(us) exclusi p(er) p(re)sentes imp(er)petuu(m). In cui(us) rei testi(moniu)m[5]

8. sigillu(m) meu(m) apposui .Dat' apud lutt(ur)worth p(re)dict(a) xxvj° die mens(is) Januarij. Anno r(egni) r(egis)[6] henrici septi(m)i t(er)ciodecimo

9. Hijs testib(us) Thoma lynch tu(n)c Balliuo de lutt(ur)worth Thoma Wygyn de ead(e)m. Rob(er)to Gardenar' de ead(e)m

10. cu(m) mult(is) alijs

Translation

To all the faithful of Christ to whom the present writing will come Henry Welle, son of the late William Welle of Bitteswell, (sends) greeting in the Lord everlasting. Be it known that I have released and completely for me and my heirs quitclaimed to John Welle of Bitteswell and Margaret, his wife, all the right and claim that I had, have or in any way will be able to have in the half part of one messuage with its appurtenances in the township of Lutterworth situated in the high street between the lord's tenements on either side and it abuts upon the highway towards the east, which same half part of the messuage I had of the gift of Agnes Welle, my mother, so that neither I nor my heirs nor anyone else in our name will be able to demand, claim or pretend to any right or claim in the aforesaid half part of the said messuage with the appurtenances but shall be excluded from every action of right and claim by the presents for ever. In witness of which thing I have set my seal. Given at Lutterworth aforesaid on the 25th day of January in the thirteenth year of the reign of King Henry the seventh. These being witnesses, Thomas Lynch, then bailiff of Lutterworth, Thomas Wygyn of the same, Robert Gardenar' of the same with many others.

NOTE

1. The common method of abbreviating *Christ* (see also Plate XI, l.11). It derives from the Greek form, the letters *x* and *p* representing *chi* and *rho* in the Greek alphabet.
2. The extreme abbreviation of *salutem* as a word occurring in a common phrase.
3. A common method of contracting *vel*.
4. Initial *u* for *v* still being used interchangeably with *v* (see next word). It is quite rare at this date.
5. Considerable contraction by a single superior letter.
6. Extreme abbreviation of common words.

FOR FURTHER STUDY AND REFERENCE

E. Maunde Thompson, *Introduction to Greek and Latin Palaeography* (Oxford 1912)
Includes transcribed facsimiles.

C. Johnson and H. Jenkinson, *English Court Hand, A.D. 1066 to 1500* (Oxford 1915)
Detailed study of the evolution of court hand, writing materials, methods and kinds of abbreviation; illustrates and discusses the forms of individual letters, signs of contraction and suspension, numerals, punctuation, etc. Bibliography. Facsimiles (in separate vol.) and transcripts.

N. Denholm-Young, *Handwriting in England and Wales* (Cardiff 1954)
Thirty-one plates of facsimiles (six transcribed). Bibliography.

L. C. Hector, *Handwriting of English Documents* (London 1958)
From medieval period to 1830. Fifty-two pages of facsimiles with transcriptions, notes on abbreviations, numerals, punctuation, etc. Bibliography.

Hilda E. P. Grieve, *Examples of English Handwriting, 1150–1750* (Essex C.C., 2nd edn., 1959)
Thirty pages of plates with full annotated transcripts and translations; two alphabets. Bibliography.

M. B. Parkes, *English Cursive Book Hands, 1250–1500* (Oxford 1969)
Twenty-four pages of plates with transcriptions illustrating the development of cursive hands during this period. Bibliography.

C. T. Martin, *Record Interpreter* (London, 2nd edn., 3rd imp., 1949)
Dictionary of Latin and French abbreviations; glossary of Latin words; Latin forms of names.

A. Cappelli, *Dizionario di Abbreviature Latine ed Italiane* (Milan, 6th edn., 1961)
Dictionary of Latin and Italian abbreviations. Nine plates with transcripts. Although based on Italian manuscripts a useful reference book.

R. E. Latham, *Revised Medieval Latin Word-List* (London 1965)

R. Kelham, *Anglo-Norman Dictionary* (1779)

F. Godefroy, *Dictionnaire de l'Ancienne Langue Française* (Paris, 1881–1902; reprinted 1938)

Eileen A. Gooder, *Latin for Local History* (London 1961)

TABLE OF SIGNS

Contraction and Suspension	Modified Letters	Runes
1 ‒ ⁀ ‿	1 p̄	1 đ
~ ⁀	2 ꝑ	2 þ
2 ⁊ ꝺ	3 ꝑ	3 þ
3 ꝯ	4 ꝑ	also
4 ℓ	5 q̄	4 ȝ
5 ᷑	6 q	
6 ; ꝫ	7 ꝙ	
7 ÷	8 ꝙ	
8 ⁊ t	9 ꝩ	
	10 f	